WHO ARE YOU CHARLIE BROWN?

A search for family

by

Wendy Brown

First published by Zeus Publications 2011
http://www.zeus-publications.com
P.O. Box 2554
Burleigh M.D.C.
QLD 4220
Australia.

The National Library of Australia Cataloguing-in-Publication

Author: Brown, Wendy, 1947-

Title: Who are you Charlie Brown? : a search for family.

ISBN: 978-1-921919-03-9 (pbk.)

Subjects: Brown, Wendy, 1947-

Brown family.

Immigrants--Western Australia--Biography.

Western Australia--Genealogy.

Great Britain--Genealogy.

Dewey Number: 929.20994

ACKNOWLEDGEMENTS

I gratefully acknowledge all those who helped me along the way, whether by encouragement or simple curiosity. To those who helped in a more concrete way, in particular the people referred to in this book by their first names, my everlasting gratitude.

To Judy and Michael, I owe you a particular debt of gratitude because of your contributions in seeking out documents and your genuine commitment to my quest. I was particularly thrilled to be able to meet you in 2007 and buy you lunch.

To Michael ('Dr Watson'), who has been a self-confessed willing slave, your emails have delighted me and not only brought me closer to my family than I ever thought possible, but created a friendship which I hope will last at least long enough for me to buy you another lunch in London.

To my cousin, Liz, without you I may never have had the enthusiasm to stick with it. Being able to share this journey together was wonderful.

To my cousins – Judy in England and Dot and Kerry in America – thank you for your stories and wonderful photographs.

To my parents, thank you for putting up with all the questions and supplying some of the answers.

To family historians who read this book, may you find in it a spark of encouragement to keep you going, despite the brick walls you will inevitably encounter. To others, may it inspire you to search for your family knowing you can indeed achieve a great deal, despite having very little to start with.

AUTHOR BIOGRAPHY

Wendy Brown was born in London and arrived in Australia in 1950 with her family of 'Ten Pound Poms'.

She has two sons, a dog, a Bachelor of Arts degree in Social Sciences, a Graduate Diploma in Business, and various certificates in training, teaching English and funeral celebrancy.

Her first book was a collection of over 100 inspirational poems, verses, sayings and quotations for use in funeral ceremonies. She and a colleague compiled, edited, and self-published *Words of Comfort* in 2002.

Her chronicle *Who are you Charlie Brown? – A search for family* is a tribute to her grandfather, who was born overseas, orphaned, raised alone in an English workhouse, and made his own way in the world from the time he was a very small boy. "The deprivations and loss suffered by this quiet and gentle man deserve to be validated, and the best way I could think of to do that was to try to find out about him, his family, and the true story of his life."

She has been researching her family history on and off since 1992 – in England, through personal contacts, and via the internet from Perth. During that time she has given presentations at the State Library of Western Australia, the Western Australian Genealogical Society Inc, and various community groups on topics relevant to social and family history.

Now retired, she produces a quarterly newsletter for her local history centre, organises monthly seminars and information sessions and volunteers her time assisting others with their own family research. She has also started on her second chronicle of the Brown family.

I saw behind me those who had gone,
and before me those who are to come.
I looked back and saw my father,
and his father, and all our fathers,
and in front to see my son, and his son,
and the sons upon sons beyond.
And their eyes were my eyes.

Richard Llewellyn
'How Green was My Valley', 1939

with best wishes
Wendy

1

Contents

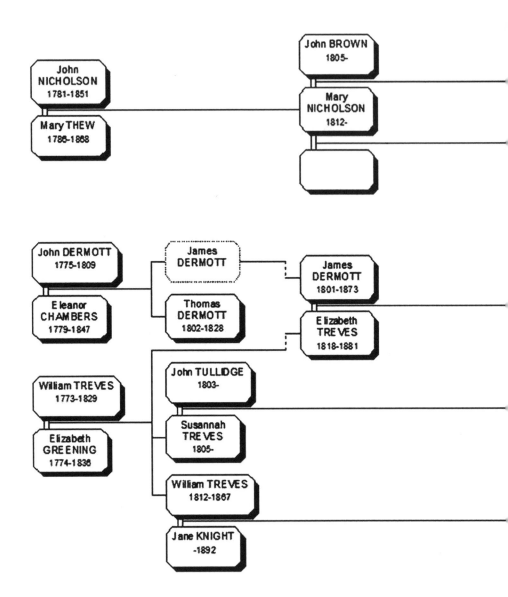

John BROWN
1805-

John
NICHOLSON
1781-1851

Mary
NICHOLSON
1812-

Mary THEW
1786-1868

John DERMOTT
1775-1809

James
DERMOTT

James
DERMOTT
1801-1873

Eleanor
CHAMBERS
1779-1847

Thomas
DERMOTT
1802-1828

Elizabeth
TREVES
1818-1881

William TREVES
1773-1829

John TULLIDGE
1803-

Elizabeth
GREENING
1774-1838

Susannah
TREVES
1805-

William TREVES
1812-1867

Jane KNIGHT
-1892

4

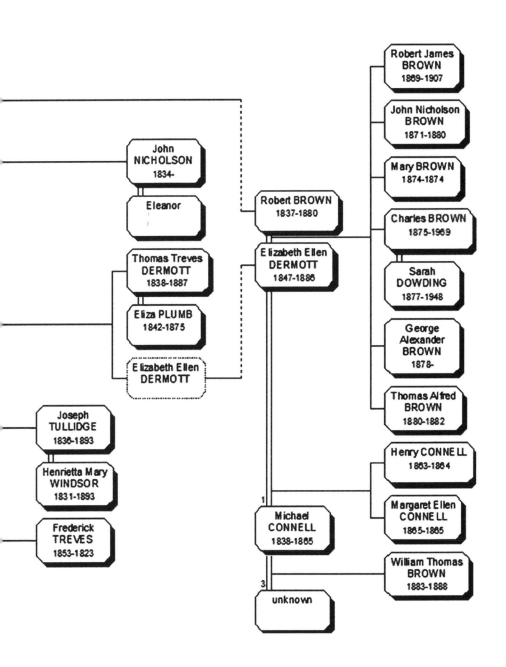

1. Roots

In all of us there is a hunger, marrow-deep, to know our heritage, to know who we are and where we came from.

Alex Haley (1920-2004)

I never knew much about my grandfather Charles Brown. I can only remember meeting him twice – once in 1954 when the family made a return trip to England and once on a solo trip I made in 1966. He was then in his 90s and still living at home. I was taken to visit him by my uncle, with whom I was staying before I ventured out to make my own life in swinging London. He was living in the same house in Kingsbury the family had moved to in the 1930s and, as I walked down the path, I saw the huge hydrangea bushes I remembered from when I was a little girl. On my earlier visit there in 1954, he had picked three of the blooms and given them to me, and they had filled my arms.

It was with a mixture of eagerness and trepidation that I entered the house in the wake of my uncle, and from the hall heard him say, "You'll never guess who's come to see you!" I presented myself to the dark sitting room and saw my grandfather sitting in an armchair, wearing grey trousers, a collar and tie, and napkin. The napkin was to protect his clothes from the ashes of the pipe he still smoked. There was a tiny black and white TV set in the corner of the room, which I knew from the family had problems with its screen, and the picture had been adjusted to about the size of a postage stamp with wide black borders. I didn't have time to take in anything else. Grandad took one look at me and said, "That's Gus' girl."

My father was always called Gus by his family, even though his name was Alexander. He was the youngest and the eighth child born, although only seven lived. The kids wanted him called Augustus, being the eighth, but they were not to have their way and he was named after King Edward VII's wife Princess

Alexandra, whose birthday fell on the same date. Nevertheless, unofficially, he was Gus.

The old man was spot on! The last time he'd seen me I was only seven, and before that he hadn't seen me since I was a baby. Perhaps it was true what my father had said when I was heading off to England on my own. Worried about meeting my family for the first time since I was a small child, I spoke to him of my concerns. Would I like them? Would they like me? Would we get on? Would I recognise any of them? He told me not to worry. He said, "When you open the door, it will be just like looking in a mirror."

I gave this man, my father's father, the tin of 'Digger Shag' pipe tobacco I had bought for him (Dad told me he'd always smoked that brand) and we exchanged pleasantries. I don't remember what about now, except there was a good deal of joshing from my Uncle Jim, who always called me his niece from 'the Antipodes' and feigned surprise that I didn't look like an Amazonian woman warrior. Everyone in the family had a wonderful sense of fun, and coming originally from the East End of London, had that quick Cockney wit and gallow's humour. Grandad chuckled when Jim complained about having to come and see him and that he would be relieved when the old man finally died and he didn't have to do it any more. One thing I still remember from the visit was that my grandfather wanted to assure me that when he died, my father, even though he was in Australia, would still receive his share of the estate.

Charles Brown died on 20 July 1969 – the day before the first man walked on the moon.

In later years, in my search for information about the family, I often wished that I had had enough interest at 19 to ask him about his life, instead of telling him about mine. Really, though, as it turned out, I don't think it would have made my search any easier.

The family story had it that he was born in India on 1 August 1875, the son of a soldier (regiment unknown), who died overseas. Notes from my Uncle Jim to his daughter Judy gave the following information:

Information obtained in general conversation with father Charles Brown –

My father stated that his father James Brown was in the Indian Army and that he died overseas when my father was about 7, and that he with his brother and mother were sent back to England and that his mother died on the journey, he distinctly remembered seeing her 'laid out' in his words with her long black hair all around. He then said that he, with his brother was placed in 'Anerley House'. His brother, who was older than him then left the house, coming back later to see him. He thought that he had joined the Army since he was in a red uniform.

This was the same information my father had. After the deaths of their parents and when they arrived in England, the two boys were sent to a workhouse. My mother thought that the boys were only about a couple of years apart in age, and my father said that when the older brother left the workhouse, he told Charles to "Get a job in food because everyone has to eat." Wise advice.

Charles went on to become a baker and worked for J Lyons & Co at Cadby Hall in Hammersmith all his life. He never missed a day's work and he was only late for work once – the first day of the General Strike in 1926, when he had to walk from Kentish Town to Hammersmith. He did not go to either war because, as a baker, he had a reserved occupation. He retired late, working through to the end of WWII. My mother also remembered that there was some to-do about him trying to get a government old-age pension because he didn't have a birth certificate and couldn't prove his age. He did get one eventually, and on his retirement from work, his employers offered him his choice of an ex-gratia lump sum payment of £200 or £1 a week for the rest of his life. He took the £1 a week and was still drawing it when he died nearly a quarter of a century later.

And that was all I knew about him. But he intrigued me. His young life must have been unimaginably hard: an orphan bought up in a Dickensian workhouse. How had he survived? What deprivations must he have suffered? How did he and his brother cope with the loss of their father, their mother, their home, their lifestyle in India, to end up in cold, wet, strange England? These were things I really wanted to find out. I came from this stock. And what of his brother? Did he survive to marry and have children? Were his grandchildren looking for their grandfather's brother, wondering if he had survived to marry and have children? Were we looking for each other? Well, regardless of whether anybody was looking for me, I was going to look for them.

It was a bit daunting to think that I, here in Perth, Western Australia, would be embarking on a task that meant getting access to overseas records and information. The only assistance I thought I might have was if one or other of my cousins knew something my father did not. I didn't know how to contact most of them and some I hadn't ever met. It was very odd: in many cultures, these cousins were people who would have been almost like siblings and yet they were, at best, just shadowy figures from my childhood.

When in England in 1966-7, I had only stayed with my Uncle Jim and his wife, and knew his daughter Judy who was a couple of years younger than me and still at school. I had met no other cousins. I guess as a 19-year old, hot on the heels of an errant boyfriend and dying to get to London, I didn't have much time for visiting aunts and uncles and family I had never seen or couldn't remember.

In 1992 I managed to meet a couple more of my relatives – my Dad's sister Lucy and her daughter Janet, who lived near where I was staying. I met up again with my Uncle Jim but not with Judy. I never knew her as an adult, and she remained a schoolgirl in my memory. Apart from that, the rest of the family were a mystery to me, until another cousin Marion, an offspring of my dad's sister Lil, came out to Perth with her husband in 1999. They had visited Australia a couple of times but had never before come to Perth. My memories of her were rather hazy, although we had often visited her home when we were in England in 1954, and it was very exciting meeting up for the first time in 45 years.

It could have been this meeting that stirred her sister Liz to come out for a visit – that or the fact that my father had been back to England a couple of times in the 1980s, re-kindling his family ties. While there he did things with his brother Jim, like visiting their old haunts – where they lived and where they played – and tried to encourage others of the family to come to Australia for a visit. Our family had been '£10 Poms' and, unbeknown to us, Liz had wanted to emigrate as a youngster but was forbidden to do so by her mother. Then marriage and family intervened, and the dream died.

Eventually, and not until she had retired, Liz decided to come for a holiday. Finally, in the southern spring of 2000, I met my soon-to-be fellow investigator for the first time since I was seven. We hit it off straight away, so much so that she returned two years later and we did a tour of the northwest together. It was during that time that I asked if she was interested in finding out more about the family, and she jumped at it.

Liz couldn't add to the information I already had, in fact she knew even less than me about the Browns. I asked her if she thought our other cousins might have more – they being older and having spent all their lives in England – and was quite shocked to find that she had lost contact with them all. This baffled me. How could people who were related and living so close, lose such complete touch with each other, when my dad and I, 20,000kms away, had more contact with them than they had with each other? It brought home to me how important being connected was for me, and I added putting all the family in touch with one another to my 'To Do' list.

The only set of cousins I or my father wasn't in some form of contact with was his oldest (and favourite) niece and her two brothers. Fortunately, Dad had kept a letter from her that she had written to him back in 1984 after one of his return visits to England, and she had used notepaper and an envelope stamped with the name of a business with which she was connected. Using the internet, I found that the business was still going, and while I had no idea whether there was anyone there who would either know my cousin or have a contact address for her, it was worth a try. Despite a false start or two, one morning I discovered in my Inbox an email from a strange address. Opening it up I read two lines of type telling me that the sender was indeed my cousin, who was amazed and delighted that I had found her.

The email of course was forwarded to Liz, and she immediately christened me 'Holmes', after the Sherlock variety. It stuck and we started signing our emails either Holmes (for me) or Watson (for her). So, armed with what scant facts we had and a copy of our grandfather's marriage certificate, which our Uncle Jim had sent my father in 1984 after his attempts to delve into the mystery of the Brown family, Holmes and Watson went searching for long-lost family.

2. Relative Strangers

But a stranger in a strange land, he is no one:
Men know him not – and to know not is to care not for.

Jonathan Swift (1667–1745)

His marriage certificate was the only official piece of paper we had with our grandfather's name on it. He and Sarah Dowding were married on Christmas Day 1901 in Bushey, Hertfordshire, where her family came from. He was living in Millwall, London, and she at Bell Cottages in Bushey. Their witnesses were Frederick Dowding and Olive A Dowding – no one from the Brown side, obviously. We didn't know who Olive was, but this was clearly a family name, as my father had a sister called Olive who died when she was quite young, and Liz's first name is Olive (which, by the way, she hates).

The big question was: did we have any living relatives we didn't know about? Had Charles' older brother married and produced children, and if he had, would we be able to find them? I started quizzing my father more closely about his family. There were the usual stories of course, but they were really about his siblings, not his parents. The only really new thing my father told me was that he remembered an Uncle Fred who lived with them for a while when he was a small boy. He remembered him because he had played a trick on my dad one Christmas, telling him that when the Christmas pudding was brought into the room, you had to stand up, salute it and sing. When the pudding made its entrance, up jumped my dad and started singing, but no one else jumped up and he was very embarrassed. That experience had stuck in his memory for the rest of his life. There was also a dwarf in the family apparently – on his mother's side. Hmmmm.

I thought Uncle Fred could have been the older brother but Liz said her mother always referred to the brother as 'long lost', so if he had been living for some time in the home, as my father insisted, he wouldn't have been 'long lost'. I bowed to her

13

inescapable logic. The family had always had boarders, so it could have been one of them. In those days, boarders and others who occupied the family home were often called 'Uncle' or 'Aunt'. Nevertheless, I found the image of Uncle Fred quite intriguing and well worth keeping in mind.

Thankfully I was not a complete novice to this family history stuff. On my last trip to England in 1992 I had done some research on my mother's side of the family. Her maiden name is Eyre, and her aunt and uncle always insisted that their family was related to the Eyres of Derbyshire, whose family tree had been traced back to 1066. While I was in England it seemed like a good chance to follow this up. That saw me spending many hours in the local library looking at the records produced by the Church of Latter Day Saints (the Mormons), and to this day I have pages and pages of transcriptions from the parish records on the Derbyshire Eyres – all in minuscule print on A3 paper. What I found out was that we weren't related to the famous Eyres at all, but that's another story. Still, that experience gave me a starting point for my search for the Browns – to investigate whether the Mormons had filmed any records of births in India.

I joined the WA Genealogical Society, which fortunately was not far away, and I found out that the Mormons had indeed microfilmed the records of baptisms, marriages and deaths in India and I could go to their family history centre and order them. I wasted no time in doing so and ordered films of baptisms for each of the three Presidencies from the years covering the period I was after, and then cooled my heels until I was notified they had arrived. When I got the call, I raced off to spend several hours going over and over them and extracting all the Charles (and Frederick, just in case) Browns that appeared. Then I sat back to have a look at what I had.

Baptisms

Bengal			Vol	Folio
1876	Brown	Charles H K	155	49
1878	Brown	Charles Frederick	63	69

Madras				
1873	Brown	Charles F	54	62
1873	Browne	Frederick M	54	143
1875	Browne	Charles V	60	154
1876	Browne	Charles S	57	202
1879	Brown	Frederick C	60	231

Bombay				
1872	Brown	Charles G	56	245
1873	Browne	Charles S A R	47	132
1873	Brown	Charles J R	47	337
1874	Brown	W F E	48	250
1875	Brown	Ernest F	49	142
1876	Brown	Charles	50	130
	Browne	Charles G S	50	289

I couldn't be at all sure I was going to be successful because I had learned with some concern that compulsory registration of births in India hadn't come into force until 1888, well after my period of interest. Nevertheless, of all the names recorded I thought I had a likely suspect: Charles Brown, baptised 1876 in Bombay. I thought this was quite a hot chance because there was some confusion as to whether my grandfather was born in 1875 or 1876. Although the family thought it was 1875, his marriage certificate from the end of 1901 pointed to 1876 because it stated his age as 25. If he had been born in August 1875 he would have been 26. Later on I learned not to be so pedantic about people's ages!

How was I going to find out if this Charles Brown was my grandfather? I decided to email the India Office in England and ask if they would look at their records for me. I had the name of Charles' father from his marriage certificate – *James Brown, deceased. Soldier* – so I was looking for Charles Brown, son of James. I thought that being from Australia might be helpful in this instance because, as I was so far away and unable just to 'pop in' and look at the records myself, someone might take pity on me and have a look for me. I was lucky and within a few days I got the following news from a very helpful man at the Oriental and India Office Collections (OIOC), as it was then called.

<u>Charles Brown</u>
Said to be born:	*10th May 1876*
Baptised at Deesa:	*25th May 1876*
	Son of Hugh and Alice Brown
Abode:	*Deesa*
Father's Profession:	*Sergeant, 83rd (County of Dublin) Regiment of Foot*
Ceremony performed by:	*Revd. P. Salinger*

I also made searches in our Ecclesiastical Records for the baptism of Charles Brown in 1876. I did find two children by that name, although the surname was spelt BROWNE. I checked the returns but neither the dates nor the names of the father matched your grandfather's details. I should point out however that these records are by no means complete and we believe we hold around 80% of returns for the period 1698 - 1947.

This Charles Brown, being the son of a Hugh Brown, was obviously not ours, and I too had checked the Chaplains' Returns and Regimental Births for India. No likely Charles Brown was recorded as born in India in 1873-1879. Dead end.

Not to be deterred, I returned to the intrigue of Uncle Fred whom I felt certain was a clue. I started to quiz my father about him and asked whether he could remember anything specific. I got just a few bits and pieces because my father's memory of his young life at home was very patchy. "Uncle Fred," he said, "was short and sort of hunched over – not a hunchback, but like that. Mum and another woman nursed him and they had to keep the door closed when he had one of his turns because he used to throw off all the bed clothes." I asked him about these 'turns' and he said his mother told him that Uncle Fred was suffering from some

16

disease he picked up in India. I asked him what he thought the disease was, and he replied that he assumed it was syphilis. Other than that he could throw little light on the mysterious Uncle Fred.

I did have one other chance to get additional information. Dad had kept in contact with his brother Jim's daughter Judy, so I sent a note off to her asking her if she had any additional information from her father or from any further investigations she might have done off her own bat. She had made some perfunctory enquiries and sent me copies of the emails she had sent to various UK government departments enquiring about our grandfather and his family. She had tried the National Army Museum for information on his father James Brown; Anerley library for possible leads on Anerley House; the British Library for Indian Army records; and even Dr Barnardo's Homes. Grandad often said he was a 'Barnardo's boy', but that was a sort of generic name given to many orphaned children and it didn't necessarily mean he had been at one of the Barnardo homes. She also added:

> *I reckoned the best way forward was to find out deaths at sea – which will be recorded in the Public Records Office or the Port of London Authority. Dad told me several times his father told him his mother died on a boat and he described how she was laid out. Then we will know where the boat came from and where the soldier – James Brown, came from.*

And a day later:

> *Grandad told my dad that he went to Anerley House with his older brother Frederick. He said he was a Barnardo's boy. Fred left and he only saw him once again when he came to visit and he was dressed like a soldier.*

That was the first I had heard specifically that Charles' brother was indeed called Frederick. I knew Uncle Fred was worth keeping in mind ... 'long lost' or not.

17

I emailed Liz regularly to keep her in the picture and to share my frustration at not being able to pin my father down with anything more. Emails between the two of us were as good as conversation, now that we had actually met each other and found out how very much alike we were – maybe not in looks but certainly in character. I wrote:

> *I'm trying to get a handle on dates from Dad about Uncle Fred and when he died. It's a bit like trying to pick up a jellyfish in chopsticks but I persist! Do you know when his sister Olive died? It seems as if it might have been in 1929 as Dad linked her death as being very close to when the Graf Zeppelin came over London (it did a round the world trip starting Aug 1929). They were living in Leighton Rd then, having moved from Willes Rd sometime about 1925. Dad remembers looking out the window in Willes Rd to see a picket line of sorts about a train carrying coal... you see, this is the type of information I get!*
>
> *This might jog a memory or two of what you heard from your mother about 'the early days'. Anyway, Dad thinks Uncle Fred died before Olive but while they were at Leighton Rd ie between say 1925 and 1929...*

That gave me some sort of end date to work to. One of Dad's sisters, Olive, had died of peritonitis when he was a child, and he thought Uncle Fred disappeared from family life about the same time. As Dad was born in 1920, I thought I would look up the death indices for a Frederick Brown who died between 1925 and 1929. Easier said than done!

I went to the Society's library and claimed a microfiche reader. Then I started looking. After six and a half hours I was practically blind and almost suicidal. I just couldn't find a suitable candidate for Uncle Fred. I was also looking for the death of Olive Brown, Dad's sister. Eventually I tracked her down, working backwards from 1933 when, according to Dad, the family had moved out of Kentish Town and into Kingsbury. Uncle Fred definitely was not around then. It turned out that Olive had died in 1931, not 1929, and in Hammersmith, not Kentish Town – but I still hadn't found any trace of Frederick. I couldn't believe it would be so hard. A lot of energy expended, eyesight ruined (probably permanently), and still no sign of Uncle Fred. Oh well, scratch him for the time being.

While I was at the Society I had also searched for Frederick and Charles Brown in the Consular, Ecclesiastical and Army Chaplains' Birth Indices but there were no Charles or Frederick Browns in India in the right years. I had searched for the death of a James Brown in the Consular Death Indices and found four: one in the Oran district files between 1876 and 1880; a J Brown who died in Suez; James Brown who died in Civita Vecchia (sounded like Italy to me); and a James Taylor Brown who died in St Thomas district (wherever that was). It was in pure desperation that I was searching the Consular Indices because I hadn't found anyone in the Army Chaplains' Death Indices – except a James Brown who died in Sierra Leone while serving with the 1st West India Regiment.

Uncle Jim had found this record and claimed him as Charles' father when he first delved into the records looking for the family in the early 1980s. He tried to follow up the regiment but there was some mystery about it, according to him, and he had left that line of enquiry to pursue his mother's family, the Dowdings. He sent copies of Dowding birth and marriage certificates to my father in 1984, and while we were pleased and surprised to receive them, and Jim's musings, we did nothing about them and they remained in the envelope they came in for nearly 20 years.

Despite having found this James Brown in the records, there was no evidence that he was ours – apart from his name; that he was a soldier; and that he had died in 1882, which tallied approximately with the family story that Charles had been about six or seven when his parents died. This man might have been my great-grandfather – but just as easily might not. I couldn't link him to our family in any way at all. He was out in Africa, not India, and I did not believe that there was only one James Brown in the British Army who had died overseas.

I also tried for marriages of James Browns in the Chaplains Returns for Overseas Marriages and got six, but I didn't really know what to do with them. Did I order the certificates? If I did, what would they tell me? Nothing that would link them to my grandfather, that's for sure. I just had to have more information.

Birth and death records had got us nowhere, and we sorely needed some success.

3. Dead Ends

A door opens to me.
I go in and am faced with a hundred closed doors.

Antonio Porchia (1895-1968)

I had had my fill of finding nothing in the overseas or London records so I decided to take another tack. I figured there would be fewer Browns who were buried at sea than were buried on land, so I turned my attention to deaths at sea, checking not only the indices of the General Register Office (GRO), which holds records of all the births, marriages and deaths in the UK since 1837 when civil registration started, but also the entries of the Registrar General of Shipping and Seamen (RGSS), which were supposed to hold all the records for people who had been born or died at sea. A large percentage of RGSS entries had never been passed to the relevant Registrar's Office, so we also needed to check the so-called Miscellaneous Foreign Returns, Foreign Registers and Returns, and Miscellaneous Foreign Deaths. Separately, Liz and I checked what records we had access to for all deaths for the surname Brown but as we didn't have a clue what our great-grandmother's first name was, it was a hopeless task.

Going through those records was very sad. So many deaths – mainly male of course, as not many women travelled. Many were unknown and unnamed. We came across entries such as *adult Brown* or *male Brown* and one *Ma Brown*. Being in the Bs, we also had just *Baby* or *Boy* with no surname at all. Despite the efforts of ourselves and a couple of other people who also searched, we had an equal amount of success with both sets of records – none!

Again, the records were not complete. I found out from an information leaflet that *passenger lists for the period before 1890 had not survived in England, with the exception of a few relating to vessels arriving in the UK between 1878 and 1888,* which are held at The National Archives in Kew. Readers were also informed: *It is advisable to know a ship's number or name and port and date of sailing before starting a search.* So, as we knew none of those, that rather put paid to the idea of searching passenger lists.

In desperation I wondered if I could find the actual ships' logs in which captains recorded the daily happenings on board ship. I doubted whether they still existed. I couldn't imagine that even the British would have kept the handwritten logs of every voyage on every ship registered in a country that had the world's mightiest shipping fleet at the time. I was grasping at straws.

Around this time I received an email from Peter Bailey of the Families in British India Society's (FIBIS) mailing list, which I had joined hoping to garner more information about this most foreign of areas to me. He was asking for volunteers to do some transcribing of records of ships and their passengers arriving and departing from India, for a project they were doing for the British Library, starting in 1853. Well, this was right up my alley. We were looking for our poor, widowed great-grandmother who died on board ship on the way to England from India. I often imagined her as her young son had seen her – laid out, with her black hair all around – and thought what an indelible image that must have been for this poor child. We hadn't found her on the lists of deaths at sea but nevertheless were determined that if she could be found, we would find her. This project might be one way of doing that because, when all the lists were finished, we would be able to search on the name Brown and see what came up. I volunteered!

Well, you know what they say... never volunteer! I just didn't know what I was letting myself in for. I put my name down and was sent a few pages of instructions on how to classify what I was going to be sent. The information was to be transcribed onto a spreadsheet, and we were given strict instructions about what to put in each of the columns. It all seemed pretty straightforward. I thought that this would be a worthwhile project, providing me with an opportunity to do my bit for the genealogical community and add to the online information that was available. I eagerly waited for my packet of papers to arrive from the British Library.

When I got my parcel, I was staggered... 28 x A4 pages of shipping arrivals and departures for 1857 from the 1858 *New Calcutta Directory*, all in tiny type.

Extract from the New Calcutta Directory 1858

Dr. Parker, Messrs. Guthrie, Garstin Thomas, Beckwith and Sanderson, Revd. Mr. McCarty, Major Eyre, Miss Durand, Mr. and Mrs. Blunt, Messrs. Cayenova, Avionalet, Goodenough and Hickey, Mrs. and Miss Fitzwilliam, Major Miles, Sir John Cheape, Dr. Holman, Major Barrow A Clerk, Lieut. Cannons.—*Second Class.*—Messrs. H. Rose, B. Phillips, T. Kelsey, H. Long, H. Hopewood, R. Townsend, Magistrate, Stewart and Mrs. Pinun.

4th.—H. C. Steamer *Hooghly*, G. T. Wright, from Singapore, 13th, Malacca, 14th, Penang, 17th and Rangoon, 27th January.—*Passengers.*—Mrs. Wyall, Mrs. Wexham and Mr. Fountaine.

R. M.—S. S. *Scotland*, G. T. Atkins, from London, 11th Nov., Cape, 18th December, Mauritius, 7th, Point de Galle, 24th, and Madras, 30th January.—*Passengers.*—*From London.*—Mr. and Mrs. Clay, Misses Ingles, Madden and Liberty, Messrs. Charles, Westcott and Cameron, Mesdames Trotter and Hutton, Mr. Hutton, Revd. Sturrock, Mrs. Sturrock, Revd. Firmenger, Messrs. Liberty and Osborne, Mrs. Fermenger, Lieutenant Trotter, Messrs. Hutton, Bell and Neuville.

All ships and ships' captains' particulars, the titles and names of first- and second-class passengers and associated persons, departure and arrival dates and places, and sundry other information all had to be typed into separate columns on my spreadsheet. This was a mammoth task which I could do for only a limited time each session, and I wondered if I would ever finish it. I did, but it took me a while. When it was complete I had 6072 lines of information.

One thing I did grasp through participating in this project, was that my original hope of being able to locate Mrs Brown through these transcriptions was highly unlikely to be realised. She would have to have been travelling 1st or 2nd class to be named. If she was travelling with a regiment, she was likely to have been an also-ran.

Not even ships' crews were named, only the captain, and there were quite a few mentions of what I came to think of as non-passengers. They included for example: *340 troops and 1 woman;*

13 Europeans, 8 women and 8 children; 1 native officer, 40 sepoys; 219 Non-Commissioned Officers and men; and even *8 bullock drivers, 20 elephants and 54 bullocks.* Sometimes there were listings for the military, for example: *110 Rank and File, 10 women and 9 children of the 8th Regiment;* and *87 men, 14 women and 22 children of the 88th Regiment;* but unless you were an officer, an officer's wife or a 1st or 2nd class passenger, you were not named.

I didn't dream my great-grandfather was ever an officer. In those days it was extremely expensive to become an officer because, until after the Crimean War and the subsequent Royal Warrant of 1871, commissions were bought. There was a scale of fees depending on what branch of the military you wanted to get into. The Infantry was the cheapest, but at the beginning of Victoria's reign, it was still 17 times the officer's annual pay.

Prices of Commissions in 1837 as laid down in Army Regulations

Commission	Price	Annual Pay
Ensign	£450	£27
Lieutenant	£700	£41
Captain	£1,800	£106
Major	£3,200	£189
Lt. Colonel	£4,500	£265

I didn't believe the family had any money, otherwise you can bet there would have been relatives to welcome the poor beneficiaries – oops, I mean orphans – when they arrived in London.

Knowing my list of shipping wasn't going to get me anywhere, I tried another tack. I joined Rootsweb's mailing list *The Ships List* and tried for some assistance there, retelling the tale of the two brothers, orphaned by the death of their soldier-father overseas and the death of their mother on board ship. I thought someone might have some idea of what could have happened to them when the ship finally docked. I didn't even know where it had docked. I had presumed it would have been at the East or West India Docks along the Thames, but I picked up from somewhere on my internet searches that they only loaded and unloaded cargo there, not passengers. The other alternatives were Tilbury or Southampton, and from there how on earth did Charles get to Penge in Surrey?

Nobody seemed to be able to help me.

4. First Success

When you make the finding yourself – even if you're the last person on Earth to see the light – you'll never forget it.

Carl Sagan (1934–1996)

What I hadn't known about when I'd done my previous research on my mother's family, and what I hadn't had cause to consult in 1992, were the UK censuses. Not only was there a system of civil registration of births, marriages and deaths in the United Kingdom, separate from records held by the parish churches, there was also a national census of the population taken every 10 years. From 1851, the census contains details of every individual who spent the night at a given address, including their name, relationship to the head of the household or institution, marital status, age at last birthday, gender, occupation and birthplace. Through the census I had the chance to find my grandfather and track his location every 10 years. If I couldn't find his birth, then at least I could find out where he had lived... a paper trail testifying to his existence. These records are so valuable to people trying to trace their family that I vow I will never balk at filling out a census form again. Unfortunately, census records are kept confidential by the UK government for 100 years, so I could only search for him on the 1881, 1891 and 1901 censuses.

I knew his name, age, place of birth and occupation, and despite the British census forms showing very little other information I thought I could pin him down. Although I was in Australia and a long way from Kew in London, where the UK census returns are held, I did have a computer and access to the internet – something my Uncle Jim didn't have when he made his first forays into the records in search of our family.

I started with the Mormon website *familysearch.org*, where I had free access to the 1881 UK census. I logged on with unbridled optimism. That lasted about 20 minutes – until I failed to find likely candidates for the orphans Charles and Frederick Brown. I

26

mollified myself by accepting that they probably weren't in England at that time. That seemed reasonable, considering that my grandfather would have been only five then, and he had said he was about seven when his mother died.

The next step was to try the 1901 census, which had not long been released and was free to search on some internet sites. I found no Charles Brown, baker, born in India, but I did find a Charles Brown, baker, born in Bushey, Hertfordshire. He was boarding at 39 West Ferry Road, Millwall, in southeast London. Was this him?

Now my grandmother's family, the Dowdings, came from Bushey, and Charles was courting her at the time. I knew they married in Bushey in 1901, on Christmas Day (that way you got the bells for free), so I checked their marriage certificate. His address at that time was 39 Stafford Street, Millwall. I went to my trusty 1992 copy of the London A-Z street directory, which was falling apart, but there was no Stafford Street. There was, however, a Strafford Street that was just around the corner from West Ferry Road. Surely this was him! Being a baker, Charles always worked at night, so it's likely he didn't give the information to the census taker himself, and if others in the household knew that he was seeing someone from Bushey, they may have thought they both came from the same place and gave the wrong information. Anyway, there was no one else who matched, so Liz and I claimed him as our grandfather.

This left us wondering about where Charles might have been at the time of the 1891 census. From someone or somewhere, I had found out that I could access this and other UK censuses if I subscribed to a website called *ancestry.com*. I couldn't get my credit card out quickly enough!

Ancestry.com opened up a world of possibilities for me. With my subscription, I could search all the UK censuses – and a lot of other English records besides.

Within minutes, I had found him – Charles Brown, born in India, working as a baker's assistant, and living with a family of bakers called Provins at 332 York Road, Wandsworth. I was absolutely thrilled, and couldn't wait to print out the record and take it to show my father. I felt a more solid connection to my grandfather through that piece of paper than I would ever have believed possible. I felt I had just won the lottery!

Now, when you are looking hard in one direction, you miss other things. I had naturally shared my discovery with cousin Liz and together we congratulated each other. She had purchased the 1881 census on CD and had been spending her time going through it with a flea comb, determined to find Charles and Frederick if they were there to be found. They weren't, but she had also taken on another project to find the family of her daughter's partner who, it turned out, also had connections with India, and she was busy with that, so it is perhaps understandable that she missed a little coincidence.

On the 1891 census, Mr James Provins was the head of the household in which our grandfather was living, and he had been born in a place called Misterton in Somerset. It is a very small village, and we know this with certainty because Liz actually lives there. It was literally years later that she realised the connection. She then traced Mr Provins through previous censuses and found that the house he lived in as a child, unbelievably, was the house at the top of her road. She can see it from her front door! I think this was more a lesson than a coincidence, and we should have learned from it. Nothing is too small to investigate, and if I had followed that advice from the start I might have saved myself some angst further down the line!

Now we had three documents that mentioned our grandfather – a marriage certificate and two census entries – but they didn't bring us any closer to finding long lost relatives. Speaking of these, it was not only the Brown side of the family that was a mystery to us. Our grandmother's family, the Dowdings, was also a mystery.

According to my father, his mother had been one of 17 – yes, that's right, 17. Her father she had described as 'one of the tired kind', and we understood that he rarely worked, believing the Lord would provide. Well, the Lord must have provided because the whole family travelled from England to America and back again, albeit steerage, and all of them except my grandmother returned once more. My grandmother had been so seasick on the trip that she vowed and declared she would not set sail again. We knew that the Dowdings had returned to settle in Rhode Island because my Uncle Jim, who was in the Fleet Air Arm during WWII, had visited some of them there when he was based in the West Indies. He said they all looked like his mum.

Buoyed by my success with the 1891 and 1901 UK censuses, I thought I would try to trace some of the Dowdings. It was more than just pure curiosity – or even the thrill of the chase. It was because I wanted to see if I could work out the name of Charles Brown's mother by looking at naming patterns. It is well known that names run in families, and naming conventions were often used. One common practice was to name the 1st son after the father's father; the 2nd after the mother's father; the 3rd after the father; and the 4th after the father's eldest brother. Daughters might be named using the same pattern but from the mother's family instead of the father's. If I could find out where the names of my father's sisters came from, that might lead me to our grandmother's name.

The enormous social changes brought about by WWI saw the fashion of naming children after grandparents, uncles, aunts and parents go out of style a bit, but nevertheless I thought it was worth finding out where my uncles' and aunts' names came from and bringing that side of the family into the fold.

5. Pieces of the Puzzle

*Puzzles are like songs - A good puzzle can give you all the
pleasure of being duped that a mystery story can. It has surface
innocence, surprise, the revelation of a concealed meaning
and the catharsis of solution.*

Stephen Sondheim (1930 -)

My father's three brothers were called Charles Frederick, Robert George and James John. His three sisters had the names Lilian May, Olive Annie and Lucy Ellen.

To trace the origins of their names I started with their mother Sarah Dowding (my grandmother and Charles' wife). As she was born in 1877, I searched the 1881 census and found her, her father Frederick, mother Lucy, and two older siblings (also called Frederick and Lucy) living in 54 Fern Street, in the Poplar district of East London. The parents had named their eldest children after themselves, the first sign that I might be on to something with the naming thing.

Next up was the 1891 census. I could find no trace of them but that didn't mean they weren't there. In the process of getting census information into online searchable databases, many errors can occur. Individuals' details were initially recorded on census forms known as household schedules, then these were copied by enumerators into notebooks. The information then had to be transcribed into databases, and indexes created from those databases. Errors can occur at each of those steps. As an example, searching for my mother's family in Derbyshire, I came across one individual who had been transcribed as living in 'Sengalora'. When I saw the digitised entry of the page in the enumerator's notebook, I could see the entry should have been transcribed as Longstone. Looking at the enumerator's style of handwriting, I could see how someone not familiar with the area had made the mistake. The '*L*' had been taken for an '*S*'; an open '*o*' read as an '*e*'; a closed loop on the bottom of the '*s*' as an '*a*', etc. Also,

30

spoken names can be misheard and recorded incorrectly. In another example from my own family, Mary Deayton (pronounced Dee-ton) was recorded as Mary Deacon on her marriage certificate.

As the Dowdings did not readily appear on the 1891 census, I thought they might have been in America by then. I asked my father if he knew when his mother's family went to America but all he could give me time-wise was that his mother had been warned about Jack the Ripper, who was operating (excuse the pun) in their neighbourhood. That meant the family was still in England and living near the Whitechapel/Spitalfields area in the East End of London in the latter half of 1888.

I did find some of the family on the 1901 census, however. Searching for Sarah I found both her and a younger sister Olive Annie – surely the Olive A, who was witness at her marriage. This was more evidence of names being perpetuated in the next generation. Sarah had named her second daughter Olive Annie, after her sister Olive Ann. Sarah and Olive were patients in the Watford Isolation Hospital. Sarah was a domestic and Olive a nurse. I couldn't find their mother, and that remained a mystery for years until I eventually found her recorded in 1901 as being with a couple in High Street, Bushey, where she was listed as a 'monthly nurse'. I hadn't found her earlier because her birthplace was listed as 'Walberton' instead of Watford and her age had been recorded as 18. A close inspection of the record itself revealed a badly written 4 that looked like a 2 but was transcribed as a 1. In reality she was 48, not 18.

I found their father Frederick recorded as an invalid with no occupation (obviously still 'tired'), and living in Bushey, Hertfordshire, with his nine-year-old daughter May, who according to the census, was born in *'Radlville,^{Con}S,S,A'*.

Well, I looked up my atlas and could not find any place by the name Radlville. Nor could I find Radville, Radeville or Radelville. I did find a Radleville in Saskatchewan, Canada, just north of the border with North Dakota, but that was in the middle of North America and a long way away from Rhode Island. And what if

SSA stood for Steam Ship of America? Was 'Radlville' a ship? If not, what or where was it? It certainly wasn't in Rhode Island.

As I had found children older than Sarah, belatedly I went back further in the census records – back to 1871, before Sarah was born. I knew Frederick Dowding and Lucy Barnett married in December 1870 because I had a copy of their marriage certificate my Uncle Jim had sent. I started there and thought I should find out where they were in 1871 and then go forward in a more systematic way. The newly married Lucy was visiting her parents and some of her siblings in Bushey, Hertfordshire, on census night, and the family included a three-month-old grandchild, recorded as Esther Jane Barnett. As Esther was the name of the eldest Barnett daughter, I took this child to be her illegitimate child. It was only when I was checking another source for all the children of Frederick and Lucy Dowding that I found that Esther Jane was actually their first child – born in Bushey and baptised on 29 January 1871. She died in the second quarter of the next year, poor tot. As her father Frederick was nowhere to be found on the 1871 census, and his next child was not born until October 1873, I thought he might have gone to America and come back again between 1871 and 1872. Possible? Maybe.

I thought I might be able to pick up the family through the Ellis Island website, which was free – a bonus – and lists immigrants to New York from 1892 onwards. I found 148 Dowdings. There were a couple of F C Dowdings (my Frederick didn't have a middle name) and two Misses Dowdings around the same ages as the girls I was looking for, but nothing really matched. The family must have gone to America before Ellis Island opened in 1892, so I would just have to try and find them on the 1890 US census.

That meant coughing up for a global subscription to *ancestry.com* or going every day to book an hour at a time on a computer at the genealogical society. I couldn't bear to do that, so it was out with the trusty credit card, and with a big gulp I hit the 'Pay' button and started searching. I was looking for a Dowding family with at least two Fredericks, two Lucys, one Sarah and one

Olive, all in Rhode Island between the end of 1888 and the beginning of 1901.

I was absolutely delighted with the American records.

The American censuses are taken at the beginning of every decade – that is 1860, 1870, 1880 etc, which certainly made it easier for me to calculate ages. Their forms were also much more detailed than the UK ones. I was not delighted however, when I found out that the 1890 census had been almost totally destroyed by fire! I went straight to the 1900 census and I couldn't find them on that either… they must have gone back to England before then. Oh no, don't tell me I had another dead end on my hands! And having paid out all that money, too. What to do, what to do?

Well, not one to be put off too easily, I thought I would check out *ancestry.com*'s immigration records, as they seemed to have loads of them. I searched for Sarah Dowding, as I thought there would be fewer of them than either Lucy or Frederick, and found her, with her mother, and sister Olive... and brother George! A find! I hadn't known she had a brother George. They were passengers Nos 5, 6, 7 and 8 on the *Adriatic* that sailed from Liverpool via Queenstown, Ireland, and arrived in New York on 4 May 1889. I joyfully shared the news with my mother that I had found Sarah's brother, only to be met with a neutral look and the words, "Yes, she had a brother George." Arghhhhh!

They were in the after-steerage section of the ship and had just one piece of luggage each. We knew from the family that our grandmother was very seasick on the voyage – either on the way over or on the way back – and that conditions were pretty dreadful for those passengers in steerage, or '3rd Class', who were, incidentally, the most lucrative cargo of all for the shipping companies. By the time my family went, conditions had improved somewhat compared to the early days of transatlantic travel. The improvement had been brought about, not through an altruistic desire to improve the condition of the human cargo, but because immigrants had to pass a medical to be allowed to stay in America and if they couldn't, the shipping company had to bear the cost of taking them back home.

The *Adriatic* accommodated about 800 steerage passengers plus 50 in 1st class, and after a refit in 1884, a further 50 in 2nd class. Single men and women were kept well apart, with married couples and families forming a barrier between them. It was expensive to travel, and many immigrants to the United States had to sell up all they had to make the journey to the unknown. Why did the Dowdings go to America in the first place? From what I had heard of Frederick the father, he wasn't a real go-getter. I was quite fascinated by this question but put it aside for investigation at a later date.

Well, I had found out about some of the family but where were Fred senior, Fred junior and daughter Lucy? If the mother and three younger children were sailing alone, I thought that the father and the older two had probably gone on before.

I found only one possible match for Lucy in the immigration records – a 'Lucie' Dowding – and despite the spelling, the right age, and by the looks of it, travelling alone. The records were pretty hard to read but she was passenger No 20 on board the *Celtic* – a 15-year-old spinster in compartment No 5 with one piece of luggage, who arrived in New York on 26 November 1888 from Liverpool, some six months before her mother and younger siblings.

I tried for either or both the Fredericks and got just one possibility, passenger No 181 on board the *Teutonic* – Fred Dowding, a lad of 16 travelling forward steerage, who arrived in New York on 9 September 1890, 18 months after the rest of the family. It just didn't seem sensible to me though, that a lad of 14 or 15 would have been left in England when the rest of the family travelled halfway around the world, presumably to start a new life in America. I couldn't find Frederick the father at all.

Knowing that spellings and transcriptions are often suspect, I did a search on 'Dow?ing', which would bring up names such as Downing and Dowling as well as Dowding. Well, I got a hit with a Frederick and Fred J Dowling, who were on board the *Germanic* and arrived in New York on 13 July 1888, four months before Lucie and 10 months before the rest of the Dowdings. This made sense to me. The father and oldest son, well old enough to be a worker, would have gone first to find work and somewhere to live. Lucy went next – as a 15-year-old – certainly old enough to be a worker, and perhaps her father and brother had found work for her. When all were settled, the rest of the family, mother and the children too young to work, followed. I felt I had my family.

So, assuming my hypothesis was correct and one or more of them were in America between July 1888 and the end of 1889, and so would have been on the destroyed 1890 census, could I find any other record of them?

Because of the virtual lack of a US census in 1890, records had been assembled from other sources that might assist people like me to find relatives around that time. Searching on the name Dowding, I came up with entries in both Rhode Island and Connecticut directories. Now that rang a bell... Connecticut. Could young May Dowding have been born somewhere in Connecticut, USA? Back to the atlas. Connecticut is right next to Rhode Island, so, cutting to the chase, I looked up the directories to see if there was a Frederick Dowding in Connecticut. Yes, there were two of them in fact – and in a place called Rockville. Well that was it of course, not Radlville but Rockville. It was another transcription error with the '...ock...' being transcribed as '...adl...'. Carefully I checked all of the Connecticut directories that were available (1889, 1890-91, 1891-92 and 1894) and teased out all of the Dowdings.

Combining the entries from that five-year period, I identified the following: William and his wife (later widow) Elizabeth, William junior, George, George W C, Frederick, and a Frederick who had moved to Rhode Island. Were these men fathers and sons? They could be.

Dow William E., farmer, h Grand av
Dowding Elizabeth, widow William, h New England av
  Frederick, rem to Providence, R. I.
  Frederick, emp Am. Mills Co., h 8 Webster
  George, h 63 Village
  George W. C., loom fixer R. Mfg. Co., h Ward n
    Union
  William, emp H. Co., h 39 Talcott av
Dowling David, bds Vernon Depot
  Fred, emp R. Mills Co., h Vernon Depot

Going back to what I knew of father Fred, it still bothered me why he would up-stakes with his family of six (known) children and go halfway round the world to America, and why to Connecticut? Now knowing that there were a number of Dowdings in that part of the world, I thought perhaps they might be related and he had gone because a relative had told him it was a better life over there. Chasing that thread, and knowing that I had to sort the Dowdings in America into who might have been the family I was looking for and who might not be, I went first to the research my Uncle Jim had done on the family. He had traced the parents of a Frederick Dowding, but that Frederick had been born in Trowbridge, Wiltshire. I knew from the censuses that our Frederick Dowding had been born in Greenwich. No go there.

Our Frederick Dowding turned out to be the youngest child of William Dowding and Sarah Hayward, who did come from Wiltshire originally. Their first three children were born there but the last five were born in Greenwich, Kent. Frederick had three older brothers, Stephen, William E and George. Ah-hah again! More examples of a child being named after someone else in the family. Frederick's first daughter Esther Jane was named after Lucy's elder sister; the second after Lucy herself; one son was named after his father Frederick; another after his father's brother George; and a third daughter – my grandmother Sarah – was named after her father's mother.

William Dowding was a name from the Rockville directories, so I looked for his marriage and the births of his children. Did he marry an Elizabeth and have a son William? Yes! And both Williams were rope makers. How about George then? George married an Anna and their eldest child was George W C. Bingo! It looked like I had them, too. Their second child was Frederick J, so it was likely that he was one of the Frederick Dowdings in Rockville, which left one unaccounted for. Was he one of my two? To be sure I had to check the previous US censuses for the Dowdings in Rockville.

Fortunately, the US census forms state not only where someone was born, but also whether they were an 'alien' when they arrived in the country. By following up the immigration records, I found out that 28-year-old George was the first of the family to go to America, and that he and his wife and their first two children, George W C and Frederick J, went in 1871 on the *City of Paris*. Both Georges were 'fullers' in the cloth industry – workers who clean usually woollen cloth of its oils and dirt – and, according to the 1880 US census, they worked in the gingham mill in Rockville. They were followed first by George's nephew William J, who went in 1884 at age 24, and then by George's younger brother Frederick and family – my family – in 1888-89. I felt I had really nailed the family link to the Connecticut Dowdings. It had taken a lot of determination and very hard work.

Time line for US emigration

1828	William Dowding marries Sarah Hayward in Wiltshire
1836	Son William E Dowding born in Trowbridge, Wilts
1837-41	Family moves to Greenwich, Kent
1843	Son George Dowding born in Greenwich
1848	Son Frederick Dowding born in Greenwich
1870-71	George and Anna Dowding and their children, George WC and Frederick, move to America and settle in Rockville, Connecticut, where the rest of their children are born
1884	William E and Elizabeth Dowding with their son William J move to America and settle in Rockville, Connecticut, where the rest of their children are born (including another Frederick!)

1888-9   Frederick and Lucy Dowding and their children Lucy, Frederick J, Sarah, George and Olive move to Rockville, Connecticut, where the rest of their children are born.

So far, I had found seven of Frederick and Lucy Dowding's reputed 17 children: Esther (deceased), Lucy, Frederick, Sarah, George and Olive, all born in England, and May, born in Rockville. I thought I would check brother George in the 1901 UK census because I hadn't picked him up there when I had located the rest of the family. I plugged in his name and approximate birth year and had a look at what came up.

Another surprise! He was there all right – and at the Watford Isolation Hospital, like his sisters, but in the male section – and with a younger Dowding – Robert. Robert was 12 years old and born in America, making it odds-on that he was George's younger brother. He was also registered as *'imbecile from birth'*. How interesting was that? So there were two children born in America, Robert around 1889 and May around 1892.

There didn't seem to be any others that I could find, and I had accounted for eight children, not 17. Now I could look to see what names in the Dowding family were common with names in the Brown family. Well… all of them were, except for Sarah herself, and little Esther, who had died long before Sarah was born.

Fred and Lucy Dowding's living offspring	Charles and Sarah Brown's offspring
Lucy	Charles Frederick
Frederick J	Robert George
Sarah	Lilian May
George	Olive Annie
Olive Ann	Lucy Ellen
Robert	James John
May	Alexander

The only additional boys' names were James, John and Alexander. James was the name of Charles' father. We knew where my father Alexander's name had come from, but there didn't seem to be any Johns in Sarah's family, unless Frederick J's middle name was John. The only additional girls' names were Ellen and Lilian.

Having a look at the families that Sarah most likely had contact with in Rockville, I saw that Frederick's brother George's 3rd child was called Lillian. She was born in Connecticut in 1872, which would have made her five years older than Sarah. Maybe Sarah became close to her and named one of her daughters after her. Certainly possible: but nowhere in the Dowding family could I find an Ellen. Could Ellen have been the name of Charles' mother? Ellen was a very popular name though, and we were speculating – but we didn't have anything else to go on.

Liz went back to the records to search in two directions: for an E Brown among the deaths at sea, and for a James Brown marrying an Ellen, surname unknown, among the marriage records in both India and England. I couldn't bear the thought of going through them again myself, having had virtually no success despite hours and hours of trawling, so I decided to try the workhouse connection.

6. The Workhouse

The boys and girls who are inmates of the Workhouse shall,
for three of the working hours, at least, every day, be instructed in
reading, writing, arithmetic, and the principles of the Christian
religion, and such other instruction shall be imparted to them as
may fit them for service, and train them to habits of usefulness,
industry, and virtue.

Poor Law Commissioners order

The one **certain** piece of information we felt we had was that Charles Brown had gone to Anerley House in Penge. Anerley was the common name for the North Surrey District School, a workhouse school holding about 600-800 children from a number of different Poor Law Unions. He said he went there, his children said he went there, and if he hadn't gone there, we believed he would not even have known about its existence. Another item of information from cousin Judy added strength to this assertion. Grandad Brown was an extremely good swimmer, which she had witnessed when they lived with him for some time, and he swam every day when given the opportunity. When we learned that Anerley House had a swimming pool, it was odds-on that he had learned to swim at school. This item of information was a complete surprise to my father, who was absolutely amazed.

The workhouse. How evocative of Oliver Twist, Fagin and the Artful Dodger – characters created by Charles Dickens. How much was fact and how much was fancy? Peter Higginbotham's wonderful website, *workhouses.org.uk*, was a terrific resource, and I became quite fascinated with the workhouse system as I tried to understand it. Parishes, unions, boards, guardians… they were all foreign concepts to me. Was Anerley House a school or a workhouse? Was it just for children or did adults go there too? What would it have been like for my grandfather, growing up there? Trying to sort this out kept me gainfully occupied for a number of months.

I found out that in 1834, the British parliament passed an amendment to the existing Poor Law Act, which overhauled the parish system of outdoor relief. This was the system of distributing either a 'dole' of money, or necessities such as wood or food, to the poor in their homes. The new Act allowed for local church parishes to come together and form a union, combining their resources to make the administration of this relief easier, and hopefully more cost-effective. These unions were usually based on existing administrative areas.

A Board was set up for each union, and local men were elected to be the Guardians in charge. The union was ultimately responsible to a central Poor Law Commission, and soon developed into a local authority for other purposes, such as administering civil registration and implementing other major government legislation relating to education, public health and hospitals. Each union therefore acted as a local executive authority for the government, and these Boards of Guardians were effectively the forerunners of local councils.

The Poor Law Amendment Act of 1834 also allowed for the expansion of the workhouse system. Workhouses or their forerunners had been run by individual parishes for hundreds of years already. By 1776, there were almost 100,000 people in 2000 parish and private workhouses in England and Wales. They were often just houses in the local parish that were used to give shelter to people, who for one reason or another were not able to fend for themselves in the outside world, even with outdoor relief – people who were sick, or old, or frail, and who had no family who could take them in and look after them.

The growing industrial revolution changed the whole nature of labour in the United Kingdom. The enclosure of common land, where ordinary people previously had 'common rights', meant that those who owned no land could no longer freely graze cattle, sheep or geese, or allow their pigs to forage, or undertake berry picking or fuel gathering; and agricultural workers flocked from the farms to the cities in the hope of gaining work in the new factories. There were more and more people who fell by the wayside, and without homes or family for support, and unable to support themselves, they found their way to the parish workhouse. By the 1830s, in many poor houses the sick were not nursed, children were not educated and paupers starved to death.

The people who ended up in the workhouse were usually too poor, too old or too ill to support themselves. For unmarried pregnant women disowned by their families, the only place they could go during and after the birth of their child was the workhouse. Often a widow's children would be admitted, leaving her free of any encumbrances and thus able, in theory, to earn her own living, but many women were forced into crime or prostitution. Prior to the mid-19th century and the establishment of public mental asylums, the mentally ill and disabled were also consigned there.

Entry into a workhouse was generally a voluntary decision but one driven by the direst of circumstances. Applicants for admission first had to be interviewed to establish their circumstances. This was called a settlement examination and was usually carried out by an officer who would visit each part of the union on a regular basis. It took me quite a while to find out exactly what a settlement examination was, and I was left shaking my head at this process of 'settlement'.

The settlement system was a central part of Poor Law management, and it had been in place since the 17th century. The first Poor Law, which came into effect in 1601 during the reign of Elizabeth I, was administered by the overseers of the poor – parish officers who were elected annually from among the more prosperous householders of the parish. The Act defined their roles and duties as the collecting of rates for, determining eligibility of, and administering assistance to the poor. A prime duty was also to prevent abuse of the Poor Law, by assistance only being given to paupers who were entitled to receive it: and the law was very specific about entitlement to aid. A person was entitled to receive assistance only from their 'place of legal settlement' and the law was similarly specific about how settlement was ascertained.

- A legitimate child took his father's settlement, which may not have been where the child was born. If children were illegitimate, their settlement was deemed to be the place where they were born, so parish overseers often tried to remove pregnant unmarried women without a settlement in that parish before they gave birth, in order to relieve the financial burden on the parish.
- A wife took her husband's settlement. A widow who remarried took her new husband's settlement, as did their children, but children from her first marriage retained their father's settlement.
- Children from the age of seven and upwards could gain settlement in the parish where they were apprenticed, providing they completed their term of apprenticeship and lived in the parish for more than 40 consecutive days.
- Servants who stayed at least one year and a day from the date of their hiring, and left with full wages, could claim settlement in the place where they were in service.
- A married man who rented a farm or smallholding, or set up as a tradesman in a new parish could gain a new settlement there – providing he stayed 12 months, paid parish rates, and £10 or more in annual rent.
- A person who inherited an estate of land and lived on the estate for more than 40 days in the year could claim a settlement there.

Under these settlement laws, the overseers of a parish could order the removal (often forcibly) of anyone who did not have legal settlement and who *might* become a burden on the parish. The normal procedure was for the person to be escorted to the parish boundary. There they would be handed over, along with the necessary documents, to those responsible for the task in the adjoining parish, who would then escort them to the boundaries of that parish. This process was repeated until the person reached their place of legal settlement. The Removal Act of 1795 amended the settlement law so that no 'non-settled' person could be physically removed from a parish unless they actually applied for relief (except the poor pregnant and unmarried woman, as she was considered the most expensive to support).

Although determining settlement was intended to prevent parishes from becoming burdened with paupers who had no claim to assistance from them, it resulted in the removal of people to parishes where they did not necessarily have any ties, or the opportunity to work. This was particularly the case for deserted wives or widows sent to the parish of their husband's settlement. When they got there, if they could not support themselves, they ended up in the workhouse. In 1846, a statute granted settlement after five years' residence in a parish or union; in 1865 it was granted after a single year's residence; but the settlement law was not finally abolished until 1929, with the passing of the Local Government Act abolishing the Poor Law Unions altogether.

After the New Poor Law of 1834, formal admission into the workhouse proper was authorised by the union's Board of Guardians at its regular meetings. In between meetings, new arrivals would be put in a receiving ward where the workhouse medical officer would examine them to check on their state of health.

Any inmate could leave the workhouse by giving a minimum of three hours' notice, or a short-term absence could be granted for someone to seek work, but in practice there was little anyone could do to prevent someone from walking out of the workhouse. These 'ins and outs' created an administrative nightmare. Each admission and discharge had to be logged, and no matter whether the admission was a new one or someone who had previously discharged themselves, the whole admission procedure had to be gone through again. To prevent unwanted comings and goings, the authorities tried lengthening the amount of notice required for discharge and even delaying the return of inmates' clothes. If anyone left wearing workhouse clothes, they could be charged with theft of workhouse property and brought before a magistrate.

Peter Higginbotham, on his website *workhouses.org.uk*, describes one such example of how the system worked – or didn't work...

In 1896, future star of the silent screen Charles Chaplin (then aged seven) briefly became an inmate of the Lambeth workhouse, together with his mother, Hannah, and his older half-brother Sydney. They went through the usual admissions procedure of being separated from their mother, the children having their hair cut short, and the workhouse uniform replacing their own clothes which were steamed and put into store.

After three weeks, the two children were then transferred to the Central London District School at Hanwell.

Two months later, the children were returned to the workhouse where they were met at the gate by Hannah, dressed in her own clothes. In desperation to see them, she had discharged herself from the workhouse, along with the children. After a day spent playing in Kennington Park and visiting a coffee-shop, they returned to the workhouse and had to go through the whole admissions procedure once more, with the children again staying there for a probationary period before returning to Hanwell.

One thing I found out was that families were often separated – not only within the workhouse but among different workhouses. If relatives were unable to support them, children went to whichever of the workhouses in the area would accept them for the lowest amount of money. If the parish had to pay because there were no relatives, siblings were often separated. In a case of two orphans from Southampton, one was sent to a large orphanage of 2000 children in Bristol, which took children from all over the country, the other to a 'shoeblack school' in Liverpool with just half a dozen inmates. In another case in 1890, relatives were separated in the Staines workhouse, Middlesex. One boy went to Canada but the other seemed to disappear. Later it was found that he had been taken out of the workhouse to be sent to Grimsby in Yorkshire and became a fisherman's apprentice at age 11.

Despite all the obstacles that we might encounter in our search – separate schools, even separate counties – there was nothing for it but to look for our boys in what records there were remaining for Anerley House. They were mainly kept at the London Metropolitan Archives (now the National Archives) but how was I going to access them from Australia? Maybe Liz could do something? Travelling to London from Somerset was expensive and time consuming, and she had two positions in the village that kept her pretty busy. I felt that, just like Princess Leia in the film *Star Wars*, I might have to send out a plea to the universe… *Help me Obi-Wan Kenobi, you are my only hope…* and that's sort of what happened actually.

7. A Good Samaritan

And so the first question that the Levite asked was:
'If I stop to help this man, what will happen to me?'
But then the Good Samaritan came by and he reversed the
question: 'If I do not stop to help this man,
what will happen to him?'

Martin Luther King, Jr. (1929–1968)

By chance, when searching the internet for references to Anerley House, I came across a person who had done quite a bit of research on workhouse records because his wife was descended from an inmate who had been sent from one to Canada. His name was Chris, and he had listed his email address on a website with the message that he was willing to do limited research on workhouse records. I jumped at the chance to ask him if he would help me and emailed him with some background and details of what I had done so far. I thought that being in Australia, I might generate an interest in this person and he might help someone so far away. I did... and he did.

True to his offer, Chris searched at the London Metropolitan Archives and came back to me with records for Charles Brown, born in 1875, apprenticed to a baker. I was ecstatic and never doubted for a moment that this was my grandfather. This is what he reported:

For Charles Brown I found only one possible candidate at
Anerley:

Name:	*Brown Chas*
When born:	*1875*
Union:	*Wandsworth*
Date of Admission:	*Aug 3 1883*
Date of Discharge:	*Sept 15 1884*

Then again:
Name: *Brown Chas*
When born: *1875*
Union: *Wandsworth*
Date of Admission: *Apr 24 1889*
Date of Discharge: *May 24 1889 (To Service)*

*I checked the Wandsworth records but surprisingly found no reference to his having entered that Union. I did come across one other reference to Charles in a **Register of Apprentices & Servants**, the details being:*

Name: *Charles Brown*
Age: *14*
Date of hiring or taking servants: *Mar 25 1889*
Name of Master or Mistress: *Mr Riddington*
Trade or other Description of
Master or Mistress: *Baker*
Address of Master or Mistress: *Blackheath*

I found no references in the schools records to any other likely Browns from the Wandsworth Union. I had a look at all likely records but found no indication of what happened to Charles' brother.

In another email, Chris went on to say he did find a Frederick Brown who was admitted in 1884, but as he was three years younger, not older, than my grandfather and came from the Lewisham Union, we really had to consider them unlikely to be connected. There were some odd things here though. Where was Charles between September 1884 and April 1889? And how come he was apprenticed to Mr Riddington in May 1889 but is then shown as being admitted to the workhouse one month later, to be discharged again one month after that? I suspected there might be two Charles Browns. It was not exactly an uncommon name. I sent my musings to Chris and, bless his cotton socks, he made yet another visit to the archives. What a gem!

> *I was back at the LMA again yesterday & spent some time going over any remaining records I could think of in the hunt for information on Charles & Frederick Brown. I have found a couple of volumes I had not been able to check before but the information gleaned probably raises more questions than it answers!*

He sent me the information he had found as a spreadsheet, and as I opened it, I saw that a Charles Brown and a Robert James Brown were admitted to the school on the same day – 21 July 1882. My heart stopped. Were they brothers? Were they my family? Names tend to run in families and two of my uncles were called Robert and James... and Charles' father was James.

From the Record of Children at the North Surrey District School 1867–1885, chargeable to the Wandsworth and Clapham Union

Name of Child	When Born	When Admitted into W. H.	When sent to School	Orphan or Deserted	Names & Residence of Child's Parents, or other relations at the time Child sent to School
Brown Robert ("James" deleted)	1870	21st July 1882	28th July 1882	O. C.	Mother, 8 Provost Street, Lambeth
Brown Chas	1877	July 21st 1882	Aug 31st 1882	O. C.	Mother, 8 Robert Street, Lambeth
Brown Chas	1877	Transferred from Westminster Schools	3rd Aug 1883	O. C.	Brother at Anerley

My elation quickly turned to despair when I read that both these boys had mothers. One mother was living at 8 Robert Street, Lambeth (on Charles' record) and the other at 8 Provost Street, Lambeth (on Robert James' record). Odd – the same street number in the same suburb and close enough in sound to be the same address. Curiosity got the better of me, and reaching for my dilapidated copy of the London A-Z street directory yet again, I looked for but found no record of either street in Lambeth. I turned to Booth's Poverty Map of London 1898-99 and still couldn't find either street. A Google search revealed in a directory a Robert Street, Lambeth, where a moneylender lived, but nothing came up for Provost Street, Lambeth. That was good enough for me. Provost Street must have been an error, and I would bet money these two were brothers.

From the records, it seemed the five-year-old Charles was sent to St James School in Tooting, while Robert James at 12 went straight to the North Surrey District School at Anerley, in Upper Norwood near Penge. A year later, Charles is recorded as being sent to the same place – with the note *brother at Anerley*. That confirmed the sibling relationship for me.

In the column headed *Orphan or Deserted* I saw the initials O. C. and wondered what they stood for. I thought it might indicate 'orphan child', as I knew that children who had only one parent were regarded as orphans, and those who had no parents as 'double orphans'. Sometime later I found out that it stood for 'other child', meaning that there was another child of the same family at the institution, and that it had no relevance as far as being a marker for children with either a single parent or none at all.

All very interesting, but that did not help me in the search for *my* Charles Brown. From what Chris had said, there were two entries in the name of Charles Brown in the Register of Apprentices and Servants.

I also found another volume of the Record of Apprentices & Servants for the boys leaving Anerley which had two entries for Charles Brown & one for Robert James Brown – all three entries showing they were apprenticed to bakers.

50

It really sounded like there were two Charles Browns at Anerley at the same time: one born in 1877 with a mother and a brother, Robert James, and the other, my grandfather, born in 1875, who had no mother but had a brother – somewhere. In an effort to really get a grasp of what was in the records, and seeing as I couldn't be there myself to look at them, I sent poor Chris back again to the school records to get me *all* the Browns that were admitted and discharged between 1882 and 1892. I was not going to give up – not when I actually had records with the name Charles Brown on them.

With the information Chris sent, I created a spreadsheet with the details of all these Brown children. I printed out many pages, stuck them together and then pored over them – when these children were admitted, where from, when discharged and how (i.e. *absconded, to service* or, frustratingly, blank). There were several sets of siblings, several references to Charles Brown, and even one to a Charles Walter Brown; and only some could be cross-referenced with other records.

Some of the entries seemed to be for the same person because the same dates were recorded for their admission or discharge. Three Chas/Charles Browns were admitted to the school at Anerley on 3 August 1883; one on 2 December 1887; and two on 24 April 1889. One Charles Brown was discharged on 15 September 1884; and in 1889, two had been discharged on 20 March, two on 24 May, and two on 1 October.

The Creed Registers in the years that I needed, which would have held much more information, were missing for surnames beginning A-B. Just my luck! After hours and hours of work it seemed I definitely had one, probably two, or possibly three Charles Browns at Anerley – all born between 1875 and 1877. Which was mine?

All reports of Admissions and Discharges for all Chas/Charles Browns at the North Surrey District School (Anerley)

Name	Age or YOB	Admission	Discharge	Comments written on the documents
Chas	1877	3 Aug 1883		Admitted from Westminster School – Brother (Robert James) at Anerley – Mother: 8 Robert St, Lambeth
Charles	8	3 Aug 1883	no date	
Chas	1875	3 Aug 1883	15 Sept 1884	
Charles		2 Dec 1887		
Charles	14		20 Mar 1889	To Service
Charles	14		20 Mar 1889	Mr Riddington of Blackheath SE, Baker
Charles	14	24 Apr 1889		From Service
Chas	1875	24 Apr 1889		From Service
Chas	1875		24 May 1889	To Service
Chas Walter	14		24 May 1889	Blank
Charles	15		1 Oct 1889	To Service
Chas	15		1 Oct 1889	Mr Thomas, Hawthorn Terr, Penge, Baker

As there were two instances of a Brown boy being apprenticed to bakers, maybe we could get a handle on who was who by tracing each of these through their work. I would try J Lyons & Co to see if they had any records of the pension my grandfather received from them, and Liz would scour the census records and directories for the two bakers, Mr Thomas of Penge and Mr Riddington of Blackheath, to see if they had an apprentice by the name of Charles Brown living with them in 1891. If they did, it would mean that there were definitely two Charles Browns at Anerley – my grandfather (who was already known to be living in

Millwall with Mr Provins at that time) and another one – possibly the brother of Robert James.

As I knew that my grandfather had worked for J Lyons & Co all his life, I looked up their website to see what I could find out. I knew about the teashops that Lyons ran and how popular they were but I knew nothing else. As usual, I went to my father to ask him. He said that his father had worked at Lyons' headquarters, Cadby Hall in Hammersmith, because he had been taken there when he was a youngster and that occasion was the first time he heard his father swear – something a young boy would certainly remember. He also knew that at one stage before their marriage, Charles had driven a horse-drawn van and he used to whip up the horses when he was outside the house in which my grandmother worked as a maid, causing her a lot of embarrassment.

In checking out the J Lyons & Co operation I learned a lot. It had 250 teashops, the first of which opened in 1894 in Piccadilly. Many were on prominent street corners in London and in other towns and cities in England – hence their popular name of 'corner houses'. Some of these corner houses though, were huge restaurants on four or five floors, where orchestras played continuously. Food and beverage charges were identical in each teashop, irrespective of locality, and so very quickly the name Lyons became associated with good quality at a reasonable price.

Lyons also undertook the Buckingham Palace Garden Parties, the catering events at Windsor Castle, London's Guildhall where the Lord Mayor's banquets were held, the Chelsea Flower shows, Wimbledon Lawn Tennis Championships and many more. Soon the company was operating hotels (which they built themselves), laundries, tea estates in Nyasaland (now Malawi), meat pie companies, ice-cream companies, tea and coffee companies, engineering works, jam and soft drink factories, confectionery manufacturing and were the first to introduce frozen food to the British public. During the war they managed one of the largest bomb-making facilities in the UK and their

engineering works made a range of war materiel. They
packed millions of rations for troops fighting in Asia and
other parts of the world and bequeathed one of their
teashops to the American personnel stationed at Grosvenor
Square.

www.kzwp.com/lyons

I asked my cousins in England for any information they might remember about our grandfather's work but didn't get much at all. It seemed that none of the grandchildren had ever had much of an idea about what he did, being either very young or not born before he retired. My grandmother died not long after the war, so stories that are often kept alive by the older women in families were not passed on to the younger generations. All I got was that Grandad was a Swiss Roll cutter at some point in his career. Also, according to my father, he baked bread for the royal family and was quite incensed that during the war they got 5% more white flour in their bread than did the rest of the population. Quite the socialist!

I made contact through the J Lyons & Co website with a man called Peter Bird and enquired with him about Lyons' pension plan, hoping to clarify the story of my grandfather's annuity when he retired after WWII. He told me that there were no surviving records but he was very interested in the story of a long-term employee of the company, and sent me a photo he had just received of the Lyons bakers in about 1906. He thought that my grandfather could be one of them. I was sure he would be too, as he would definitely have been there in 1906, working to support his wife and, by then, four young children. I was thrilled to get a picture which might show my grandfather as a young man, and I printed it out almost life-size when I got it, poring over it and trying to pick him out myself. I emailed the photo to all my cousins in England, with the request to tell me if they thought our grandfather was one of the men and, if so, which one. I was very careful to be quite neutral about it. They all sent back messages and each one of them had picked out the same man. I waited until I had all the replies and then showed the photo to my father, without giving him any other information, and he pointed to the exact same man. "That's him!" he said, and that was good enough for me. My grandfather as a young man – what a find!

J Lyons & Co's bakers in 1908.
Charles Brown – back row, last man on the right.

I kept corresponding with Peter Bird, and he sent me two more photographs of Lyons' bakers in the early days, both of which featured my grandfather. He also offered to put up an extended obituary for Charles on the Lyons' website. It had been growing in me for some time that I would really like to mark my grandfather's life somehow, and this would be perfect. All I would need to do was to give him details of who his parents were, when and where he was born, the composition of his family, when he started work with the company, what work he did, where he lived etc. All the things I didn't know. But I would, in time.

Having his obituary on the internet would be just great. He would have been tickled pink – this man who had lived nearly a full century, been orphaned and brought up in a workhouse, lived through two World Wars, raised seven children, and witnessed so many changes. In his time he saw, amongst many other things, the emergence of motorbikes, motor cars, aeroplanes, supersonic flight, space travel, telephones, radio, television, the zipper, vacuum cleaners, tape recorders, microwaves, washing machines, bakelite, the parachute, antibiotics, X-rays and sliced bread!

While all this was going on, Liz had tried to trace the bakers that the Brown boys were sent to when they left Anerley, to see if that produced some more leads. She was a demon, working at directories and census returns, trying to identify Mr Thomas of Penge and Mr Riddington of Blackheath.

She tried Mr Riddington first. What a mystery he turned out to be! It was such an uncommon name that she thought he would be easier to pin down. Hmmmm. Well, firstly, it appeared that there were two bakers called Riddington – Stephen and Thomas – but there were problems. Thomas retired before 1871, and we thought it highly unlikely he would be taking on apprentices in 1889 when he would have been 81. Worse, Stephen Riddington died in 1882, seven years before young Charles Brown was even discharged from Anerley. There were no other Riddingtons to be found in the various censuses or directories of the time. We figured that other people might have taken over the business and kept the name if it was a well-known one. Anyway, scratch the Riddingtons!

So it was off to track down Mr Thomas of Penge. Well there was a Mr Frederick I Thomas, baker, of Oakfield Road, Penge, but in 1891 he had no apprentices living with him so we couldn't eliminate any of the Charles Browns. Scratch Mr Thomas!

8. Parallel Lives

*The most exciting phrase to hear in science, the one that
heralds new discoveries, is not "Eureka!" but "That's funny ..."*

Isaac Asimov (1920–1992)

Because I was frustrated and couldn't think of what else to do, I
looked up the family of the two Brown boys, Robert James
and Charles, in the 1881 census just for interest, to see what their
circumstances were before they went into the workhouse.

The brothers were two of a family of four boys – in April 1881
living with their widowed mother Ellen, and her widowed mother
Elizabeth Dermott, at 76 Union Street, Lambeth. Lambeth was an
area of mixed socio-economic groupings according to Booth's
Poverty Map of 1898-99. Charles Booth, a noted philanthropist
and social researcher, coloured the streets of London according to
the general conditions of the inhabitants. Black was *lowest class.
Vicious. Semi-criminal.* Dark blue was *very poor* and red was
middle class. Union Street was a mixed area, with some
comfortably off, others poor.

According to the 1881 census, the 33-year-old Ellen Brown (I
told you Ellen was a popular name) was born in Wandsworth,
which explained why her two boys at Anerley were charged back
to the Wandsworth Union. By law, the constituent parishes in each
union were responsible for paying for their own poor, wherever
those poor happened to be – that's why it was so important to
establish someone's place of settlement.

Of Ellen's four sons, the eldest Robert James was recorded as
having been born in Gosport, Isle of Wight; the second son
Charles in Halifax, America; and the younger two George and
Thomas in W India. I had never before come across a reference to
W India. People who were born in India usually recorded their
place of birth either as just India, or with a place name such as
Bengal, Hyderabad or some such.

Grandmother Elizabeth Dermott died in the northern summer of 1881, and some time in the next year, Ellen and the children must have moved to 8 Robert Street. My best guess was that it was impossible for her to support herself and four children, the youngest only 18 months old, on what she could make as a seamstress, so she was forced to surrender her two eldest children to the workhouse.

While people would do just about anything not to have to enter the workhouse, it did provide a number of positives. It just depended what you were comparing it to. For these two boys the workhouse would have provided them with substantial housing, solid food, some education, and training for work – and at least at Anerley there was a hospital and separate quarters for children who had ringworm and other infectious diseases. Children were taught basic literacy and numeracy skills, and (more importantly) practical skills such as shoemaking, baking or farming (for boys), and sewing, washing and domestic tasks (for girls).

While some children's records at Anerley were very easy to follow – with one entry for admission and a matching entry for discharge – others were not nearly so clear.

Robert James' time in the workhouse school was easy to follow. Admission into North Surrey Schools on 21 July 1882, then a week later and after the normal admission routine, off he went to school. As he was 13, he would have been in the same dormitories as the men. Workhouse inmates were strictly separated, not just by gender but also by age. All the children under seven were kept together, then boys aged 7-12 were a separate group. Boys aged 13 and above joined the men. Girls only went in with the women once they turned 16. The sick and infirm were separated out again. Family groups were not kept together, and parents could only visit their children on application to the authorities. Segregation was strictly enforced, and transgressors were punished. It was certainly no holiday home.

The records show that the discharge age for children was between 14 and 17, and Robert James was discharged on 3 January 1887 at 15 years of age to a Mr John Beal, baker, of West

Wickham, Kent. Charles' record was not so clear – as we have seen.

After he was admitted to the workhouse with his brother, Charles stayed there for a month before being sent off to St James' School, Wandsworth Common, Tooting, where he stayed for almost a year. I thought that might have been because he was so young but I did see records of other children at very young ages being sent to Anerley. I was very sad that this poor little chap, possibly not yet five years old, was sent away to an industrial school, losing his older brother just a week after being separated from his mother and younger siblings. I wonder if their mother knew this was going to happen, or if she assumed that they would be kept together. Without doubt, she would have had no control over it anyway. Charles was transferred to Anerley on 3 August 1883 but would have been in a separate class of inmates and thus estranged from his brother. In due course he followed his brother into the baking industry to make his own way in the world.

After remarking to Liz how this family and ours must have had similar experiences, and wondering how many other families had been in this position, we sighed and let them go. Then with a collective deep breath, forced enthusiasm and determination, we turned our attention to the Indian military.

9. Soldiers of the Queen

It's the soldiers of the Queen, my lads
Who've been, my lads, who've seen, my lads
In the fight for England's glory lads
When we've had to show them what we mean:
And when we say we've always won
And when they ask us how it's done
We'll proudly point to every one
Of England's soldiers of the Queen.

Leslie Stuart (1864-1928)

Apart from our grandfather's marriage certificate, Uncle Jim had sent one other certificate relating to the Browns. His digging back in the 1980s, mainly on the Dowding side, had also unearthed the death certificate of Private James Brown of the 1st India Regiment Corp (West India Regiment), who died of phthisis (tuberculosis) aged 30 on 12 December 1882 in Sierra Leone, Africa. He was the same man I had found when trawling through the military deaths at the genealogical society earlier on in the piece.

While Jim had accepted that this man was his grandfather, I couldn't link them up in any way, other than that he happened to have the right name and was a soldier. Realising that we needed to be a bit more rigorous than our Uncle Jim, Liz and I had to investigate the military connection further. I started to delve into the Indian army. What a minefield! The 1st India Regiment Corps at Sierra Leone, which was known as the West India Regiment, seemed to have been made up of 'black' soldiers and a few 'white' officers, as it was thought that 'blacks' could withstand the conditions much better than your average English soldier. As I read more, I felt that this man was an entirely unlikely candidate for Charles' father. I had little else to go on except that I just didn't think he was.

I attempted to track the movements of this regiment to see if it had been in India but actually couldn't verify anything. I was also apprehensive about him being the only soldier called James Brown we had come across, who had died at about the right time. With quarter of a million men serving in India alone, there must surely have been more than one James Brown. There were of course, but as he was the only candidate we had uncovered so far, we decided that if we didn't find another, Liz and I would adopt him posthumously as our great-grandfather.

As we didn't know our great-grandfather's regiment, it was going to be a real struggle to identify him. The first thing to do was to see if there were any records that were indexed alphabetically rather than by regiment. An information sheet, *Army Other Ranks – Finding the Regiment* put out by the Public Records Office in Kew states *records of books of effects of soldiers who died give the regiment and are arranged alphabetically. The years 1862-1881 have the reference WO 25/3476-3490 indexed by WO/3491-3501.* Ah-ha... I was on to something here. It went on to say that *Description books for each soldier are in WO25/266-688 in alphabetical order in regimental volume.* There were only 422 pages of them! It would seem I would still have to go through all of them as I didn't know his regiment, but how was I going to get access to them from Australia?

I thought I would try my luck at the India Office again, so I crossed my fingers and sent an email. I got this reply:

There were two armies serving in India at this time, the regular British Army and the Indian Army which although it had native troops also had serving European (British) officers, NCOs and ordinary private soldiers.

From what you say, it sounds as if the father of the two boys could have been serving in the British Army. If James Brown had been serving in the Indian Army he may well have been out in India for some time, and when he and the boy's mother died, the children would have been placed in one of the Army orphanages in India rather than being sent home.

It is important if you can, to see if you can find out the regiment in which James Brown served as from this you will then be able to determine if he was serving in the British or Indian armies.

Worse and worse. Two armies. Not only did I not know which regiment, I didn't even know which army.

Liz and I corresponded regularly and at length around this time. She also did a fair bit of research and sent me this snippet of information from an article called 'The Unattached List' by Peter Bailey published in the Families in British India Society (FIBIS) journal:

Frequently, men who were married with a family in India, and who felt at home in that country, wished to stay there when their regiments had completed their tour of duty and were due to be posted to almost anywhere else within the Empire. One way of achieving this was to request transfer to a regiment freshly arrived in India. The alternative was to request transfer to the Unattached List. An additional advantage of the latter, apart from withdrawal from the front line, was that promotion prospects in the Unattached List were generally rather better.

In the same article, Liz came upon this example of such a transfer:

A sergeant from the 45th Foot originally signed on for a period of 9 years in 1870. With 3 years still to go, he transferred to the Commissariat Dept (Unattached list) in 1876. He was still there in 1882 when he died.

She believed that our great-grandfather's army career could quite easily have followed this pattern, and as she had found a James Brown on this list, she was going to follow it up.

We had also done some reading on life in the army around the second half of the 19th century.

During the nineteenth century only single men were allowed to enlist in the British Army and any soldier wanting to marry, had, in theory, to seek the permission of his commanding officer.

Wives of those soldiers who then received permission to marry were considered to be 'on the strength' of the regiment. This term was in use from mid-century onwards. It served to emphasise the special position of these wives as part of the 'regimental family' and the exclusion of wives not recognised as such. The Army allowed approximately 4–6% of soldiers to marry. This number was considered enough to supply sufficient women to undertake tasks within the regiment, such as washing, sewing and mending. Despite the injunctions against marrying without leave, soldiers continued to marry.

The wives of soldiers who married without permission were known as 'off the strength'. It is not known how many off-the-strength wives there were, because officially they did not exist and were therefore not eligible for any sort of welfare benefits or housing and were not recognised as army widows if their husbands died.

Before the Crimean War, those off- the-strength wives and widows who could not manage to support themselves had no option but the Poor Law. Many women resorted to prostitution, or worked in deplorable conditions for starvation wages, to avoid the workhouse. Even when outdoor relief was available, widows claimed only as a last resort, because of the risk of losing their children. Often, all, or all but one of her children, were taken into the workhouse to free a widow for work, as a condition of relief being paid.

The large numbers of soldiers' wives and widows who had frequent recourse to the Poor Law led to one of the enduring perceptions of the soldier's wife as being that of a shiftless slattern; an image which existed alongside the more generous, reformist view of the soldier's wife as one of the poor who deserved the support of the state or philanthropists. One or other of these differing views dominated or receded, depending on the country's need for its armed forces at any given moment.

Janis Lomas, 'Delicate duties',
Women's History Review, Volume 9,
Issue 1, 2000 pp123-147

We found this information quite fascinating. It was all grist to the mill, and we started to get a picture particularly of what our great-grandmother's life might have been like. Unfortunately, it didn't really get us any further forward and left us with a rather uncomfortable feeling that if our great-grandmother was an 'off list' wife, we might never find her.

In India, because of the overwhelming disparity in male and female numbers, a soldier's widow never had to wait long for a proposal. Some were even proposed to at their husband's funeral service. We wondered what this might mean in regard to our widowed great-grandmother. So many options started to raise their heads. Was she ever married to Charles' father, James? Was she Indian or part Indian? Was she Mrs Brown when she died, or had she remarried? How did she have the money to sail to England? Had he left a will? Was there a register of soldiers' wills? If she was taking the family to England, why was no one there to meet her? What happened to the brothers when they disembarked? Why did the children (Charles, at least) end up in a workhouse in Surrey and not in London? And so the questions went on and on.

There was nothing for it but to try and track down the British Army regiments that were in India at the time my grandfather was born, so off I went to the genealogical society's library. I had been directed to the reference book *In Search of the Forlorn Hope*, which for me was at once both an appropriate and depressing title. The two volumes of this publication listed British regiments under the places in the world where they were stationed, and the years they were there. From that information, I found there were 57 regiments in India in 1875 – any of which could have been my great-grandfather's. Even if I had the capacity to search the records, where did I start? It was all getting a bit hard.

10. God Bless America

Give me your tired, your poor,
Your huddled masses yearning to breathe free;
The wretched refuse of your teeming shore,
Send these, the homeless, tempest-tossed to me.

Emma Lazarus (1849-1887)

What rescued me from the depressive state into which I had fallen as a result of having zero success with the Browns on two fronts – the military and the shipping lists – was trying my luck again with the Dowdings. If I couldn't find one branch of my father's family in England, I would find the other in America.

I had already found out that Dad's mother's family, the Dowdings, had left England in the period 1888-89. Frederick the father and son Fred J went first, followed by young Lucy (Lucie), then her mother and siblings Sarah, Olive and George. I had located all but the two eldest – and I thought they might well have stayed in America. They would have been 27 and 26 by then and perhaps had married there. Frederick was living in Bushey, Hertfordshire, with his daughter May, while the four other children, Sarah, Olive, George and Robert (who, like May, was born in Connecticut), were all incarcerated in nearby Watford's St Mary's Isolation Hospital for some reason. I don't know what they were there for but it was obviously infectious. It could have been as serious as diphtheria or tuberculosis, both of which killed so many children, but was more likely to have been scarlet fever or some lesser disease because they all recovered and serious sickness was never mentioned in the family.

I didn't know when the Dowdings had returned to England but the family story had it that my grandmother was the only one who didn't go back to America to settle in Rhode Island. My mother said she seemed to remember Sarah saying she had a brother living in England, but Dad had no such memory – not that that was confirmation of anything. So it was back to examine the American immigration records once again – this time for the family's second trip to the new world. They hadn't gone until after the 1901 UK census on 31 March, and certainly Olive hadn't gone until after she was witness at her sister Sarah's marriage to my grandfather at the end of 1901. The search was on for the Dowdings from 1902.

Bless the Americans (and I don't often say that). Their records were getting better and better, and this time I uncovered a bombshell! I thought that mother Lucy might have stayed in America with her daughter Lucy, because the first time I looked, I couldn't find either of them on the 1901 UK census. I knew that mother Lucy hadn't died because father Frederick was still classed then as married, not widowed, so I was really looking for father Frederick and the rest of the children. What I actually found was mother Lucy and father Frederick, and the two youngest children, Robert and May, on a *Manifest of Alien Passengers* on board the *SS Cymric* arriving at Boston on 15 July 1906, having sailed from Liverpool nine days earlier.

What I didn't expect was that Robert, who had been classified by the UK census as *imbecile from birth*, was labelled by the American authorities as both *dwarf* and *grandchild*!

My father had said there was a dwarf in the family and now we had him... not only a dwarf, but a grandchild raised by Lucy and Frederick as their own. His mother was most likely to have been their daughter Lucy because the next oldest daughter, Sarah, didn't arrive in America until May 1889 and would only have been 12 or 13 at the time Robert was born. If Lucy was the Lucie I had found arriving in America in November 1888, it was perfectly feasible that she might have become pregnant in the New World before the rest of her family arrived in May 1889, and given birth to Robert, who then had been raised by her parents.

All were said to be citizens of the United States and they were going to join their daughter, Mrs Robert S Hoare, in Providence, Rhode Island. The notes in the last columns were quite difficult to read, so out came the magnifying glass and I read... *Ct. Court Dec. 15/93 papers of naturalization. Question of Citizenship and bastard child) (all agree to be held until case of Robert is settled).*

It also stated that Robert's occupation was *musical artist*. That was really a turn up for the books!

I had to confirm Mrs Hoare's identity but there was no doubt in my mind it was Lucy. I hadn't been able to find her on the 1901 UK census with the rest of the children, so I was double-clicking on *ancestry.com* in double-quick time. I found the marriage in 1891 of Lucy Dowding to a Richard G Hoar not Robert S Hoare, but bearing in mind that the information given to the immigration agents was not from Mrs Hoare herself but her relatives, I thought it was a good bet this was the marriage I was looking for. I also found a descendent list for the Hoars, created and posted on the website by someone (name and contact details unlisted) who was researching the Hore/Hoar/Hoare line. As I wasn't able to contact this person directly, I had to confirm their information through the only other source to hand, the US census documents. I had learned that family pedigrees had to be regarded very carefully because not everyone charting their family trees confirmed their findings by checking primary sources. On checking subsequent censuses, I found Lucy, Richard and their children as listed, so it looked like whoever had done the Hoar line had got it right. Suddenly I had Lucy Dowding Hoar's details of marriage and a named list of all her deceased descendants, plus a numbered list of all her living descendants – almost to the current day.

Lucy was married in Rockville, Connecticut, at the Union Congregational Church on 3 August 1891, two months before her 18th birthday, to 24-year-old Richard Grose Hoar of Massachusetts. Their first child was born a year later, and they went on to have 12 more.

Now I knew why the Dowdings had gone to Rhode Island and not back to Connecticut – it was because Lucy was there. So now I was starting to build a picture of Dad's mother's family. I contacted my cousin Judy, because I knew Uncle Jim had visited the Dowdings in Rhode Island just after the war, and she told me she had some photos of the American Dowdings amongst her father's things. Uncle Jim had died in 2000, and Judy, as his only child, had all his personal papers and photographs. She promised she would send them to me and I waited, very impatiently, for them to arrive. Some time later, 21 small photos arrived in a plastic display book. Nostalgically, it smelled of old pipe-smoke and it took me back to the time I was in England as a teenager when I had lived briefly with Uncle Jim's family. I was struck then by how much like my father he looked, and when I saw him light his pipe and toss the match underhand into the fire, I could have been sitting in the lounge room at home watching Dad do the very same thing. Grandad, too, smoked a pipe all his life and I think that all of his sons smoked as well. It's amazing that they all lived to be in their 80s and 90s – except for Uncle Bob, who died suddenly of a heart attack when he was 60. The men in the family were slim and of average height or taller, and the women were all short and dumpy. Sarah was less than 1.5m (only 4ft 9in). We have a photo of Charles and Sarah out walking on the promenade at Margate in 1927, and even in heeled shoes, she just comes up to his shoulder.

**Charles and
Sarah Brown
1927**

On the promenade
at Margate

When I got the photos of the Dowdings in America, I could see immediately how my father's sisters took after their aunts.

Obviously, the aunts were very close, and there were quite a few photos of them together and with their children. What was fascinating was the glimpse into the life of these people – my father's uncles and aunts and cousins – that these snapshots gave me.

The photos ranged in date from 1916 to the 1940s. I managed pretty much to work out who was who, with a lot of study and some assistance from words written on the back of them. Irritatingly, one of the photos had been cut to fit the plastic pocket it was in, thus cutting out the explanation on the back of one photo. Most of them showed Sarah's three sisters: Lucy, Olive and May, and their children. There were a couple featuring George, but none of little Robert. It was wonderful to have these happy snaps of real people – real family.

It was with great reluctance that I sent these photos back after having scanned them into my computer. I would love to have had them to keep, but understood my cousin's concern that I return them to her, as they were part of her father's legacy. On second thoughts, I should have had them copied onto photographic paper and will do so sometime in the future, but they will never be the same as the original ones... battered, creased, scratched and covered with the touches of people who had sent, received and cherished them.

Very soon I had tracked down all the marriages of the American Dowdings – Lucy (already done), George, Olive and May. Olive married Thomas Chadburn, and May a George Tunnicliff. They were a pretty easy family to find, and I traced them through the American censuses to 1930.

Encouraged by the unexpected gift of the Hoar lineage, I thought I would join the *Genes Reunited* website. At that time, a member could enter the details of their relatives listed on the 1881 UK census, and any other member who had an interest in them could make contact by email through the website. I entered all the Brown and Dowding family details from the 1881 census, thinking that maybe the curiosity apparent in Liz and me might be evident in others in the family. Somewhere, someone might be looking for us, just as we were looking for them.

One morning not long after, I opened my email, and there to my amazement was a message from *Genes Reunited* saying that a member was enquiring about my relative, May Dowding. I was electrified! I sent off the required identification and got this reply almost immediately...

> *I am the daughter of Robert F Tunnicliff, granddaughter of Dorothy Mae Tunnicliff, great-granddaughter of May Dowding... I have quite a few pictures of the Dowdings. I would like to keep in contact. I have lots of family info to share, including all the Dowding graves in RI. Lots of death and birth Certificates. I am willing to share.*

She went on to say she did not live in Rhode Island but was planning another trip there and that she had several living relatives there, including a granddaughter of May Dowding and George Tunnicliff. I honestly couldn't believe it. I was corresponding with my third cousin, and through her I had a chance to contact another cousin. And she had photographs and certificates! Who would have thought that my frustration at finding nothing about the Browns would result in me finding out just about everything about the Dowdings? I was over the moon.

All this came to me just in time for me to create a family chart for my father for Father's Day. He was brought up not knowing any grandparents, aunts, uncles or cousins. Thanks to my research, he now knew of aunts, uncles, cousins, nephews and nieces, grand-nephews and grand-nieces on his mother's side, and his family tree had sprouted like it was Spring.

Through this contact, I then got an email from my second cousin Kerry, in Rhode Island.

> *My mother was Edna, the youngest of May and George's children. Sadly, my mother Edna passed away peacefully last*

June at the age of 89. She would have been so excited to know of you.

I have been slowly restoring the photos that I have which is a painstaking process but well worth it ...

Let me know if I can help you with any info that I might have. I have to start working on this again, as I have not done anything in quite some time....unlike our cousin Dot who is relentless, and a great detective.

She had been digitally restoring a photo she had of a Dowding family she thought was my grandmother's. She sent it to me and I wept. It was my family all right – and all scrubbed up too.

I was able to send this photo to all my cousins in England, and it gave me enormous pleasure to be able to do that. We had been so scattered for too long and had so few photos, or even family stories, that I felt this really brought us closer together. That was proved to be so, because later in the story I went to England and had a cousins' reunion, where at least one cousin from each family was present, and we shared just being together for the first time in our lives.

Seeing Charles so handsome and proud in the photograph made me doubly determined to discover his story and – hope against hope – maybe some relative of his. I returned to the scene of my previous frustrations and once again entered the world of the workhouse, as this was our only real positive lead.

11. Four Years On

The greatest obstacle to discovery is not ignorance –
it is the illusion of knowledge.

Daniel J. Boorstin (1914 -)

I started again – this time with an email list covering workhouses and hospitals. These lists are joined by people who have interests in specific subjects and who use them to ask questions, give answers and generally correspond with other subscribers with shared interests. Some lists have hundreds of subscribers, possibly thousands. Using these email lists looked to be a good way of easily accessing information held by a lot of people, and anyway, what did I have to lose? The more people I talked to about my quest, the more likely I was to uncover someone who might be able to help me.

Dear List

This is my first posting.

I am looking for information on my grandfather Charles BROWN (b in India on 1 Aug 1875) and his brother Frederick, a couple of years older, who went to North Surrey District School (Anerley House). They were orphaned by their father, James, who was a soldier and who died in India (whereabouts unknown) and mother (name unknown), who died at sea on their journey to England. This would have been in about 1881-82.

I have the names of all the BROWN children admitted and discharged from Anerley House from 3 August 1883 to 1 November 1889 and I have a number of comings and goings for "Charles BROWN". I have even traced another BROWN family whose son Charles was in the school at that time, in an effort to eliminate those named "Charles BROWN" who were not my grandfather.

The confusion comes because of the comings and goings of these boys from the school. I also can not associate any Charles with a Frederick BROWN there at the same time, so I'm rather stumped.

I do not want to bore you with more details so if anyone is familiar with the comings and goings in this establishment I would be most happy to correspond with you off list.

This brought an immediate off-list reply from a lady called Judy, who said she would do some lookups for me if I wanted. What an angel! I gave her the story so far, including what I had already found out and what documents I wanted her to look at from the ones not already searched. From the online *Access to Archives* catalogue, I had made a list of all the documents held by the National Archives pertaining to Anerley House. Some that hadn't been searched were minutes and letters of the Board of Guardians; the band register; reports on boys sent to Wales; a list of visitors to children; and a register of children whose parents were not in receipt of outdoor relief. I thought this last one might yield something and hoped that my orphans might be classed in this category.

Within a couple of days, my newly acquired contact in London sent me the results of what she had found, which held nothing new, except for the weight, 3st 2½lb (20kg) and height, 3ft 9½ins (1.15m) of one Charles Brown at eight years old – by today's standards, very small and thin.

The next day, I received another long email from her, musing on whether the Charles Brown we had already discovered at Anerley was indeed my grandfather, despite the fact that he had a living mother. She invited me to look at things a little differently saying:

In NSSD 171 (Record of children 1879-1895), supposedly a consolidated list, there is after all only a single entry for the name Charles Brown.

Maybe this Charles is your grandfather and not Ellen's son at all, or even called Brown originally... Perhaps Ellen

and her husband took him in, as a favour to the boys' real
father, who might have been a fellow soldier? Perhaps this
Charles' place of birth as shown in 1881 is simply wrong?
All this is pure fantasy of course, but it is not impossible.

It was really difficult to ignore the poignant and lasting memory of a man, who as a boy had seen his mother lying dead, but putting aside all I thought I knew about the death of my grandfather's mother, I took a purely objective and rational approach. Despite the comings and goings, different ages, different years of birth, and regardless of a Charles Walter Brown being named, there was definitely only one Charles Brown at Anerley in the 1880s, who was born in the 1870s... so... regardless of whether he had a mother or not, the inescapable fact was that he must have been my grandfather. That really pulled me up short.

Judy went on to say:

I wonder if you have been able to track the mother back at
all? Is she the Elizabeth Brown found in 1871 in Woolwich,
born in Wandsworth in 1848 and married to a Robert
Brown? Have you found a Brown/Dermott marriage?

I had previously tried for a Brown/Dermott marriage when I first found the family on the 1881 census, but hadn't found one. I had searched on Dermott because that way I had a first name, Ellen, but had found nothing.

Despite the father being called Robert (not James) and the mother being called Elizabeth (not Ellen), I went scurrying back to the census records. I had already looked at the 1881 census and found Charles and his three brothers, mother (Ellen) and grandmother (Elizabeth Dermott) living in Lambeth, but I hadn't gone any further back than that, as Charles hadn't even been born in 1871. Judy had obviously gone back further than I had, and I was intrigued as to why she thought this family was mine.

I pulled up the reference she gave me for the 1871 census and was transfixed! Despite the different first names, there was no doubt this was the family I had found on the 1881 census because the son, Robert James, was there as large as life, born in Gosport less than two years previously. His mother, now named Elizabeth, had been born in Wandsworth and was the right age, and his father, Robert Brown, born in Newcastle-upon-Tyne, was... a soldier... a soldier... a soldier. There it was in black and white. He was a Gunner in the Royal Artillery!

I stopped breathing. My heart was pounding in my ears. I came out in goosebumps, and tears sprang to my eyes. In my bones, I knew this was them. I just didn't believe it was yet another coincidence. We had found them! They were there all the time and living at 15 Engineers Road, Woolwich.

It all fitted now. It was inescapable. Charles Brown: the only one born in the 1870s and at Anerley House in the 1880s; his older brother, Robert James (not Frederick, despite the references to Uncle Fred); his mother (Elizabeth Ellen as it turned out); and his soldier-father, Robert (not James) Brown. Despite the story of his mother dying on board ship, in my heart I knew we had my grandfather's family and we could finally let go of the James Brown in Sierra Leone. Grandad had named his father as 'James' on his marriage certificate, maybe because he knew his brother had one of his father's names and thought it was James, not Robert. He'd just got it wrong, the same as he had got it wrong that he had been born in India. I sped to the genealogical society library to look up the military births overseas again and found him this time – Charles Brown, born not in India but in Halifax, Canada in 1875.

I was elated – there was not a doubt in my mind that this was him. It just felt right.

12. Into the Breach

Ubique means that warnin' grunt the perished linesman knows,
When o'er 'is strung an' sufferin' front
the shrapnel sprays 'is foes;
An' as their firin' dies away the 'usky whisper runs
From lips that 'aven't drunk all day:
"The Guns! Thank Gawd, the Guns!"

Rudyard Kipling, 'Ubique', 1903

At last, maybe we had a chance of finding Charles' father through the army. To find out about Robert Brown, we just had to try again for the military connection. We didn't have any other options. It was going to be a matter of trying to find which battalions, batteries, regiments or brigades of the Royal Artillery were in Halifax in 1875 when Charles was born. We then had to marry them up with the same ones that were in India in the years following – when George and Thomas, the two younger boys were born, but before the family arrived back in England after Robert's death.

It was back to the internet searches for some information on the Royal Artillery. This was made more difficult because men of the Royal Artillery accompanied other military units. They were the guys with the guns. I rushed back to *In Search of the Forlorn Hope*, looking to see if the Royal Artillery was in India in 1875. Of course, it was – it was everywhere. That's their motto: *Ubique* – everywhere.

It was in trying to find out anything I could about the Royal Artillery and its various brigades that I discovered, on a web page about an old comrades' association, an email contact for people wanting information about men serving in regiments in Canada. I sent an immediate email, hoping for information as to where I could get records that might pertain to my great-grandfather, Robert Brown, Gunner, RA.

I saw that you were willing to do limited and specific look-ups for people in regard to regiments in Canada.

I am looking for my great-grandfather, Robert BROWN, born in Newcastle-upon-Tyne in or around 1837, who was certainly a gunner in the Royal Artillery. He was either married (I haven't been able to find a marriage record for him) or living with Elizabeth Ellen BROWN (nee DERMOTT), born in Wandsworth. They were living in Engineers Rd Woolwich with their baby son in 1871.

By tracking where his 4 sons were born, I believe he was a member of the 3rd Battalion.

Robert's oldest son, Robert James, was born in Alverstoke, Hampshire in England in the 4th quarter of 1869. The second son, Charles (my grandfather) was born in Halifax, Canada in August 1875 (although he believed he was born in India). The third and fourth sons, George and Thomas were born in "W. India" in 1878 and the 3rd quarter 1880 respectively.

From my research I have the 3rd Battalion being sent to Halifax in 1869 and then to India in 1875.

The father, Robert BROWN died in India between January 1880, when his last son was conceived and March 1881 when the 4 boys and their mother, now a widow, were back in England living in Lambeth.

If you could possibly look up the relevant record/s I would be most appreciative. If you are not able to see your way clear then I quite understand. If you would let me know one way or another, that would enable me to make what other arrangements I can.

I hope these details are specific enough for you.

The very next day I received a reply email from a man called Michael which started out:

...my partner has passed to me your e-mail with regard to Robert Brown of the Royal Artillery. I am at the National

Archives in Kew most days and will be pleased to have a look for Robert. Unfortunately, because Robert died in service there will be no discharge papers for him...however there is probably quite a lot we can find on him in the records of the Royal Artillery.

He went on to say:

To familiarise myself with the info you have provided I have spent the last hour looking at the 1851, 1861 and 1871 census records as well as the BMD registers of the GRO. I think you will find that Robert's wife, Elizabeth Ellen Dermott was married first to Michael Connell...

I was gobsmacked!

Blithely, he announced:

I will find Robert's locations during his service on Tuesday.

and followed that up with:

Robert's burial should be recorded as well as any baptisms of his children. I will have a look at these [at the India Office] next week for you... If you would like us to purchase the marriage certificate of Robert's marriage to Elizabeth, do not hesitate to ask. We can obtain them in four working days.

I couldn't believe it. Here was someone else willing to do the work that I couldn't do. Such amazing generosity from another complete stranger! This news prompted a lot of email traffic flying between me in Australia and Liz in England, eight hours behind. Many had subject lines like *READ THIS!!!!!!* and *Wake up! Wake up! Wake up!*

79

We had received a staggering amount of information in just a few hours. We seemed to have located our great-grandparents, something so distant we hadn't even thought about it when we started our search. And much, much more was still to come. Our wonderful military man took on Robert as a research project for us and spent the next week camped at Kew searching for him – tracing him backwards through the army's muster books.

True to his word, on the following Tuesday I received an email that explained that he could find no record (like us) of births of the other two children or the death of their father in India. He did find listed in the Regimental Registers of Births, however, the births of George A Brown and Thomas Alfred Brown in Bermuda in 1878 and 1880. Bermuda... not India. W Indies... not W India.

The family story was becoming more and more estranged from the family truth. We had now confirmed a family of four boys, not two: the eldest was born in England; the second, my grandfather, was born in Canada, not India; and the youngest two were born in Bermuda. We had their father called Robert, not James; a mother very much alive, not buried at sea; and it was becoming more and more apparent that there was no connection to India at all.

Looking at the time line, Michael found that it was impossible for Robert to have been with the 3rd Brigade RA, because, although the Brigade was in Canada at the time of Charles' birth, it arrived there in 1869, before his first child, Robert James, was born in England. Michael's location records showed that three batteries of the 7th Brigade had arrived in Canada from England on 3rd February 1873. They remained in Halifax until 1876, when the 1st battery left for Bermuda on 17 April, the 2nd left for Barbados on 23 February, and the 7th left for Jamaica also on 23 February. As George and Thomas Brown were born in Bermuda, it was the 1st Battery of the 7th Brigade that he needed to follow.

To give you some idea of the complexity of the military records Michael was chasing, we eventually found out that Robert originally enlisted in the 13th Battalion, but when the system changed in 1859 from one of battalions and companies to one of brigades and batteries, he became one of the 7th Battery of the 21st

Brigade and was later absorbed into the 1st Battery of the 7th Brigade, which then became the 17th Battery of the 9th Brigade!

Michael and I, as well as now having my grandfather in common, also found we had a common love of cricket. At this time, Australia and England were playing out the Ashes series in Australia, and Warnie was having a field day in Adelaide in the second test. Michael's second email to me finished:

> *This time tomorrow evening, after a visit to Kew tomorrow, I hope to be in a position to resolve the situation. Mind you if your Mr Warne bowls us out in Adelaide tomorrow, to go two up in the Ashes series, I might be too depressed to do any research.*

The next day I received an email (as I knew I would) that opened:

> *Despite being in the deepest trough of depression, brought on by you-know-who, I struggled to the archives today and found the info on Robert Brown you have been looking for. Some of the info may well surprise you. One fact being that he and Elizabeth had at least 6 children between 1866 and 1880.*

Six children, not four!

Michael had been working through the quarterly musters of the Royal Artillery. The musters showed that Robert was not admitted on to the married roll of the regiment until 4 March 1871, even though it turned out that he and Elizabeth Ellen had married on 30 May 1866, nearly five years earlier. In those days, just because you were married to an army man didn't mean that you got to travel with him. You had to be on the married roll to do that, and then only about 3-4% of married men had wives travelling with their regiment. The 7th Battery 21st Brigade musters showed Robert at Gosport from April 1869. They also showed that, although the birth certificate of his oldest son, Robert James, has him born at

Gosport on 26 August, he was actually born at a little place called Colyton in Devon. That was a strange anomaly that I skipped over, swamped as I was by the huge pieces of information that were coming my way every day now.

The family was stationed at Gosport until 1870 when they went to Woolwich, and there Robert was admitted to the married roll of the regiment. It was at Woolwich, the headquarters of the Royal Artillery, where we had found Robert, Elizabeth and baby Robert James on the 1871 census, living in Engineers Road. Elizabeth was by then heavily pregnant with their second son John Nicholson, who was born later that year on 2 July. John Nicholson was a child we knew nothing about, although as there was a six-year age difference between my grandfather Charles and his older brother, we thought there might have been other children in between. There were two in fact – John Nicholson, and a daughter Mary who was born in Canada the year before my grandfather, and lived just 13 days. John also died as a child, only nine years old, in Bermuda in 1880.

So, a whole different set of family circumstances was being unveiled. We now knew our grandfather's mother had been married before, to a Michael Connell, plus two of his older siblings had died, one before Charles was born. I doubt whether Grandad had known much, if any of this. In those days, and even much later, not a lot was talked about to children, and he was so very young of course. Surely, he would have been fascinated to hear about it in such detail!

Information on Gunner Robert Brown continued to roll in. Michael traced him back to 1863, before his marriage, when he was shown at Fort Monckton, Gosport. There is a series of Royal Artillery books of births, baptisms and marriages up to 1877 for the 7th Brigade that has survived, and these record Robert's marriage to Elizabeth Ellen Connell at Ashford, Middlesex, and the baptisms of their first two sons.

The Bermuda musters record the names of the parents, and the ages (not the names) of their children in years and months. From them we were able to match the ages of the children to the GRO regimental registers, which recorded their names, birth and baptism dates. While they were in Bermuda, the two youngest children George A and Thomas Alfred were born. It was not until I got their baptism certificates that I saw George's middle name was Alexander – my father's name! I was absolutely delighted by that. Dad only had one name, whereas all of his siblings had two. His brothers and sisters were Charles Frederick, Lilian May, Robert George, Lucy Ellen, Olive Annie, and James John. Alexander didn't really fit with the rest of the names but all could now be linked to someone in their parents' families. Dad may have been told he was named after King Edward VII's wife Princess Alexandra, with whom he shared a birthday, but having unearthed the rest of the family I like to think that he was named after his uncle, George Alexander.

The final piece of the puzzle came just eight days after Michael and I had first made contact. It deserves to be read as I received it.

I have finally nailed your great-grandfather Robert. Today at the archives I spent four hours of fruitless searching, looking for the unit Robert had come from to join the 21st Brigade at Gosport in 1869. I then decided to look at the musters for the period in which Robert enlisted, only to discover that they have not survived. This was the period in 1859 when the Royal Artillery changed from Battalions to Brigades and there is a gap of around six months in the musters, which unfortunately is the time Robert enlisted. I also looked at books called "Depot Description Books" in which recruits joining the various battalions would have all their relevant details entered. Few books have survived beyond the year 1858 and those that have did not list Robert. I also had hoped to find, in the series called "Records of Service", some reference to Robert but again these books relating to all the Brigades, having survived until 1939 were then destroyed by enemy action during WW2.

It was while looking through the indexes for these books that I noticed that there were two depot description books, listed for some strange reason out of sequence, among them. One of these, for the 13th Battalion, covered the period up to the end of 1859. Although the index to the book contained no reference to Robert (it would appear that the indexing had stopped at the end of 1858), there was at the end this rather lovely entry:

Reference WO69/77 13th Battalion Recruits.
Folio No 43
No 394 Robert Brown, age 22, five feet seven inches tall.
Enlisted 12th April 1859 in Dublin by James Cook, Pensioner, for service in the Royal Artillery.
Born in England in the County of Northumberland, in the parish of St. Chalton, near the town of Alnwick.
Trade on enlistment, shoeing smith.
Can read and write.
Fresh complexion, brown eyes, dark brown hair.
Date of attestation: 13th April 1859

There is no parish in Northumberland called St. Chalton, but I think the St. is an abbreviation for South. There are parishes called North and South Charlton, just a few miles north of Alnwick and about 30 miles north of Newcastle.
It may now be possible, having a battalion number, to follow him forward. I did notice that all the entries in the book were for men enlisting in Ireland and this was obviously a recruiting party for the 13th Battalion in Ireland. After this Robert would almost certainly have gone to the RA HQ at Woolwich and been allocated to another unit.
Although it may not be possible to complete the chain to the 21st Brigade, I do think this is your great-grandfather.
Enjoy the read.

I read it and re-read it. I gave thanks to the Universe and particularly to Michael. I just sat with it – for ages – hugging this knowledge to myself, and smiling. Five feet seven. Brown eyes and dark brown hair – just like all the men in the Brown family. And a Geordie!

With the buzz of all this information coming across the world to me from London and then back again to my cousin Liz in Somerset, it was time to try and put it all down in some semblance of order to read, re-read and digest.

On 3 February 1873, Robert Brown and his wife Elizabeth Ellen and their two sons Robert James and John Nicholson arrived in Halifax, Canada, with the 1st Battery of the 7th Brigade of the Royal Artillery for a three-year posting. During their time in Canada, Elizabeth and Robert had a daughter Mary born on 25 September 1874 who, sadly, died just 13 days later. Exactly 12 months later, on 25 September 1875 (not 1 August, as he had thought) their son Charles was born. Charles was not baptised until 5 December, some 2½ months later, whereas all the other children were baptised within a fortnight of birth. I thought that this, coupled with the identical date of birth of the two children, might mean that 25 September was not Charles' actual birth date but one set down perhaps in memory of the dead daughter. In those days, birthdates were not as important as they are today, and they were often mis-recorded.

When the civil registration of births, marriages and deaths was instituted on 1 July 1837, parents were not obliged to give information on their children's births unless requested to do so by the local registrar. The registration of births and deaths was the responsibility of the registrar for each area, and not of the parents. Each local registrar sent copies of his records to the Registrar General in London four times a year. Some parents thought baptism was a legal alternative to civil registration and didn't register their child. Others just didn't bother because they didn't have to. From 1874, the Births and Deaths Registration Act allowed for fines to be imposed on those registering a birth more than six weeks after the event, and at the same time the responsibility for registering a birth passed from the registrar to the parents or the occupier of the house where a birth took place. If parents were in an isolated community, or for some reason took longer than six weeks to register a birth, in order to escape a fine they might just amend the child's date of birth when registering it.

Charles was only eight months old when the family set forth on 17 April 1876 for St George's, Bermuda, in the West Indies. He may never have been told he was born outside the West Indies, and it is very easy to confuse India with the Indies... the people who transcribed census records did it all the time. The general population also referred to India and the West Indies as East India and West India respectively.

In March 1878 Robert and Elizabeth's fourth son George Alexander was born, and in 1880 their fifth son Thomas Alfred was born.

The last half of 1880 was a traumatic time for the Browns. In June Robert was put on the injured list and hospitalised, and in July they buried their second son John Nicholson. In November Robert was invalided back to Portsmouth with his family, and he died on Portsea Island of pulmonary tuberculosis (TB) on 15 December. Elizabeth Ellen and the four boys were given a warrant to travel from Portsmouth to London, and that's where I found them on the 1881 census, living with Elizabeth Ellen's widowed mother in Lambeth.

It being so close to Christmas when I found out all of this, I thought I would send my cousins in England the information about our grandfather and how it was so different in reality from what we had always believed. I wrote up the story and sent it off with the photo I had received from our cousins in America. They were surprised, delighted and thankful. I couldn't have wished for a better Christmas present.

13. The King's Shilling

Come laddies come, hear the cannons roar
Take the King's shilling an' we're off tae war

Author unknown

The holidays gave me time to take stock and see what we had achieved.

Our original quest was to find out if we had any living Brown relatives, and that was still the core of what we wanted to do. Of course to find the living we first had to find the dead. Of Robert and Ellen Brown's six children, we knew two had died in childhood – Mary in Canada and John in Bermuda. We knew what had happened to Charles of course but couldn't find any others of the family on the 1891 census. So we started with Robert James, the eldest, who left Anerley House on 3 January 1887 at 15 years of age to go into service with a Mr John Beal, baker, of West Wickham, Kent.

The only piece of information we had about him was that Uncle Jim said Grandad only saw his brother once after they had been separated and that either he was wearing a red uniform or he was dressed like a soldier. Either way, it was a pretty fair guess that Robert James may have gone into the army. He would have known nothing but the army all his life until he was 11, when his father died. Then it was a whirlwind round of travel to London, meeting and living with his grandmother until she died, then separation from his mother and brothers and into the workhouse. I pondered over all this with Michael, and one morning got an email from him.

With regard to Robert James, I think I may have found a candidate in the army that is a possibility and an interesting story to boot. I searched the discharge registers of soldiers discharged between 1900 and 1913 without success. Plenty of Robert Browns in the infantry, as well as the RA, but none that matched Robert's place and date of birth. The discharges between 1883 and 1900 revealed again, a number of Robert Browns but only two Robert James Browns, whose details were worthy of consideration. These in fact turned out to be the same man.

The first Robert James Brown enlisted for the Royal West Kent Regiment on the 11th July 1890 and was discharged a day later, rejected as unfit due to defective vision. The age given on enlistment was 18 years 11 months and his birth place was given as Wandsworth, Surrey. The age is a couple of years out, but this is not unusual in army records and although we know Robert was born in Gosport, he may have thought he was born in Wandsworth, having lived in the area in 1881 and Anerley House is not far away.

The place Robert enlisted at, in 1890, was Shortlands and there is a Shortlands just three and a half miles from Penge.

The second Robert James Brown is shown enlisting into the Royal Artillery on 31st July, just nineteen days after failing his medical with the Royal West Kents. The details given are the same on both enlistment documents. Age, birthplace, trade given as a baker, height five feet five inches, fair complexion, brown eyes, dark brown hair, religion C of E, no next of kin shown, tattoo on left forearm with the letters CRB, are the same on both papers.

Robert also lied when he answered NO to the question "have you ever been rejected as unfit for Her Majesty's Service". Robert went on to serve 10 years before being discharged on 23rd January 1900 as unfit for further service. The reason given was debilitation, aggravated by the climate in India, where he served three years from November 1897. Robert was also being treated for secondary syphilis when he was invalided back from Rawlpindi to Netley Hospital, Portsmouth and finally discharged.

Of course this does not match up to your grandfather's story of RJ coming to see him in Anerley House before he left in March 1889 and wearing a red uniform. The Royal West

Kent regiment would have worn red, but the RA were basically blue although they had flashes of red as I understand it.

However it makes a good story.

This was fantastic news. Michael had done it again. He was right, the Poms might not be very good at cricket but some of them were fantastic at digging up dead soldiers!

We had assumed that Robert had visited Charles at Anerley but Charles left the year before Robert joined up. It is quite possible that Robert enquired after his brother though, or they may even have exchanged letters, as both of them could read and write. Anyway, there was no doubt this was my great-uncle Robert James Brown.

I went to the 1891 UK census but couldn't pick Robert up. He might have been serving overseas before he was sent to India at the end of 1897, and I was sure Michael would get whatever information there was to get on him. I was right. A couple of days later I got this follow up from him:

Just a quick Brown update. I found in the Chelsea Pension registers (WO116/172) this afternoon, Robert James Brown of the RHA, being granted a pension of 7 pence a day for 27 months, from the date of his discharge 23rd January 1900. The details the same as his discharge papers, except they give his intended place of residence as c/o Mr Walker 57 High Street, St. John's Wood. Mr Walker is probably the army agent responsible for paying pensions in the area.

I was back on the 1901 census faster than you could imagine. Now we had a chance to find him in England – somewhere in the area of St John's Wood. I found a Robert J Brown, general labourer, aged 30 (approximately right) and claiming to be born in Wandsworth, Surrey, so I checked him out. He was living at what looked to be a boarding house at 30 St Ann's Terrace... *part of St John's Wood Terrace.* Off to my tattered copy of the London A-Z and I found it. St Ann's Terrace was the extension of St John's Wood High Street, north of St John's Wood Terrace. No doubt about it. This must be him. He was alive and unmarried in 1901, living in north-west London when his brother Charles was living in Millwall. How I cursed that I would have to wait decades before I could pick him up in 1911, 1921 and 1931 – I might not even be alive then. Why couldn't the British have had the same system as the Americans – the US censuses are released after 70 years, not 100.

There was one other fascinating snippet of information I gleaned from Michael's emails. *Robert was also being treated for secondary syphilis.* Immediately my mind turned again to my father's recollection of Uncle Fred and his condition being the result of some disease he picked up in India, and the assumption he had made that this was syphilis. Coincidence? Fancy? Well, there was just no way to check, and none of us had been able to find a definitive death for Robert James.

Michael had checked:

> *On the death front, I have searched the indexes from 1920 to 1933 and the only realistic entry that I found was in the MQ of 1933 at Stepney, volume 1c page 382, a Robert J Brown age 65. There was also a Robert Brown age 62 at Stepney in the JQ of the same year. I seem to remember you saying your grandfather was living in Milwall at some time and Stepney is close by.*

Liz had reported:

> *Singular lack of success trying to find the death of Robert J.*
> *Have searched the death records from Q1 1923 through to Q4 1935 which should have covered it I think. Not even close. No RJBs of the right age in the right place are recorded.*

However, I did find a Robert J who died in Q1 of 1932, whose death was registered in Woolwich.

Even Judy had had a go:

Just a quick note on the subject of Robert J in 1901.

You said you had identified a possible death for a Robert J Brown in Woolwich in 1932. There is in the 1901 Woolwich census a Robert J. Brown, aged 29, born India, married to a May E. Brown. Probably another ex-soldier.

Checking the marriage index, he could be a Robert John Brown who married May Elizabeth Taylor in Woolwich in Jun Qtr 1898. He could well be the 60-year-old Robert J Brown who died in Woolwich in Mar Qtr 1932. So if you haven't yet ordered the death certificate you might want to reconsider?

While Robert's death remained a mystery, we knew he hadn't married by the time he was in his 30s, and we also knew he had secondary syphilis, so he wouldn't have been a good candidate for marriage. I thought the likelihood of him finding a woman who would marry him and have his children was not high.

All this information that Michael had got from the military records on Robert (the father) and Robert James (the son) he filmed with a digital camera, put the photos on a CD, and gave it to us when we met up later in England. Later still he managed to fill in the missing part of Robert's service, and so then we had all the information there was to have about both father and son.

We knew that Robert first joined the 13th Battalion of the Royal Artillery in Dublin, Ireland, on 12 April 1859 when he was a 22-year-old shoeing smith. He would have been marched to Cork and from there travelled by ship to Bristol, where the recruits probably boarded a train to London, then marched the nine miles to Woolwich, the home of the Royal Artillery. Robert was on leave during the second half of January 1860, then transferred to the 6th Brigade and departed for Malta and Corfu. He was overseas at the time of the 1861 UK census, returning to Gosport and Portsmouth in August that year. The next year he was promoted to Bombardier. Two years later he was promoted to Corporal, and in May of 1865 started recruiting in Darlington, Durham, which was in the Leeds military district.

A Sergeant in the Royal Artillery

In January 1866 he was moved to recruit around Staines, Middlesex, where his future wife, the young widow Elizabeth Ellen Connell was living. We don't know if he knew her before but, if not, it was a quick romance because they married at Ashford on 30 May that year, within a few months of his arrival. They only had a year together before Robert was sent again to the Leeds district, having been promoted to the rank of Sergeant.

On 29 November 1867 Robert re-enlisted for a further period of service. He was then 30, married, but with no children that we know of. Just four months later he returned to Gosport, and the next muster shows that he was in prison awaiting trial by Court Martial. He had been charged with *'producing false certificate of Mess accounts'*. He was sentenced to 84 days hard labour and reduced to the ranks.

Robert was released on 14 September 1868 as a private, and 12 months later, his son Robert James was born in Colyton, Devon, where Robert's in-laws were living. Elizabeth Ellen must have gone home to mother to have the baby. Robert was on furlough for the whole of December 1869, then in 1871 the 7th Battery removed from the coast back to Woolwich, where Robert was admitted to the married roll. His second son John Nicholson was born three months later in Woolwich, Kent, and 18 months after that, the family found itself in Halifax (now in Nova Scotia), Canada. It was there that Robert's Battery was absorbed into the 7th Brigade. From then on, we had no detailed information on Robert except for the quarterly musters, which showed the ages of his children. He was invalided home in November 1880 and died of tuberculosis 10 days before Christmas, after more than 20 years in the army, and the last nearly eight years in service overseas.

His son Robert James followed him into the Royal Artillery in July 1890, in reality 21 years of age, but somewhere during his years at workhouse schools he lost two years and was recorded as being 18 years and 11 months and a baker when he attested at Shortlands, Kent, very near West Wickham. Despite having been born in Colyton, Devon, and registered as born in Alverstoke, Hampshire, he gave his birthplace as Wandsworth, Middlesex (properly Surrey). This was his mother's birthplace and the parish that had responsibility for the family's costs while they were in the workhouse.

The first indication that Robert James might not be squeaky clean surfaced almost immediately. He had attested for the Royal West Kent Regiment but had been discharged the following day due to defective eyesight (guaranteed to be short-sightedness, which all the Brown men suffer from). A fortnight later, when enlisting for the Royal Artillery, he had answered untruthfully that he had never been rejected as unfit for Her Majesty's Service. He was 5ft 5¼ins tall (1.66m) and weighed 117lbs (53kg), with a fresh complexion, brown eyes and dark brown hair. He also had the letters CRB tattooed on his left forearm, tattoo dots on his fingers, and a scar on the back of his left thumb. Part of his attestation papers consisted of a list of medical and other conditions under the heading Primary Medical Examination. Of immense interest was a line drawn thus under some of the letters of one of the medical conditions: *abnormal curvature of spine*. Dad's description of Uncle Fred as *a small man... sort of hunched over...not a hunchback, but bent over* certainly seemed to fit Robert James – regardless of his different name.

Robert James also served overseas like his father, not in Malta, Corfu, Canada or the West Indies, but in India – from October 1897 to January 1900, when he too was invalided home. He was a driver with the Royal Horse Artillery, which meant he was around the horses a lot, and in November 1896 received a kick to his right knee which continued to bother him. That was not the only injury he received and he spent many days in hospital as a result of illness and poor health: bronchitis, gum boils, rheumatism and lumbago, contusions, nephritis, dental problems, sore throats, inflammation, Ague (malaria), conjunctivitis, gonorrhea and syphilis. He also went through two courts of enquiry, one regarding an accident off duty and one an accident on duty. No fault was assigned to him on either of these occasions, but he wasn't an exemplary soldier either, being awarded and losing good conduct pay on a number of occasions.

On 13 September 1899, Robert's detailed medical history for invaliding stated:

This man was transferred to the Station Hospital at Landour [India] *from Meerut* [where he had been in hospital for 130 out of the last 183 days] *on 22ndJuly suffering from Ague. His disease was changed to Secondary Syphilis on the 6th August for which complaint he has now had four admissions. He is very debilitated & emaciated & suffers from severe syphilitic rheumatism especially of the right knee – He has also suffered considerably from Ague. His condition is such that a change to England is necessary. The disease though not the result of direct military service has been aggravated by them but not by intemperance, vice or misconduct. Contusion right thigh in -/92 – off duty. Contusion right kneecap on duty in -/96. Neither affect his efficiency.* [His injuries were] *not attributed to exposure on duty,* [but] *aggravated by the climate of India.* [His

94

disability] *was not permanent - will be able to earn a full livelihood in civil occupation.*

He arrived at the Royal Victoria Military Hospital at Netley on 24 November 1899 and was discharged from the Royal Horse Artillery at 28 years of age on 25 January 1900, with a pension of seven pence a day for 27 months.

From not knowing anything about these two men – not even their real names, though we knew they existed – we now knew so much about them it was almost as if they were materialising before our eyes. Physical descriptions, places they had been, things they had done, privations they had suffered. Amazing really.

14. E.E.

In respectful memory of our great-grandmother
Elizabeth Ellen Brown
who died 2 May 1886 aged 40
Rest in peace

During the time when we had been trying to put off the desperately difficult task of how to go about searching the War Office records in London, Liz and I had tried to trace Charles' mother – once we knew she was very much alive when the boys went into the workhouse.

We had her maiden name (Dermott) because on the day of the 1881 census she was living with her mother, Elizabeth Dermott, at 76 Union Street, Lambeth. Both were listed as seamstresses, and not only Robert James and Charles were living with them, but also the two younger children, George and Thomas.

Judy had found the birth of Elizabeth Ellen Dermott (although the name had been transcribed in the index as Dermell) in Wandsworth in the second quarter of 1847, to Elizabeth Treves of Dorchester, Dorset, and Guernsey-born James Dermott, railway station agent, then stationmaster. Elizabeth and James Dermott also had a son Thomas Treves Dermott, born nine years earlier when they were in Ireland. I made a note to find out some time if Elizabeth was related to the famous Dr (later Sir) Frederick Treves, who performed an appendectomy on King Edward VII two days before his scheduled coronation, and was so closely associated with Joseph Merrick, the 'Elephant Man'. Treves is an unusual name and Sir Frederick also came from Dorset.

In 1851, the Dermott family were living in Ashford, Middlesex. Ten years later, as recorded on the 1861 census, Elizabeth Ellen was still living with her parents in Ashford, but her brother Thomas had left home and was footman to the Irish Earl of Wicklow, living in his house at 2 Cavendish Square, Marylebone. By this time, Thomas had dispensed with his Irish origins and stated his place of birth as Ashford, Middlesex. He went on to marry Eliza Plumb from Newbury in Berkshire, who also worked for the Earl of Wicklow at the same time as Thomas, and they had five sons and a daughter.

Elizabeth Ellen's first marriage was to a Michael Connell on 12 December 1863, when she was only 17 and already heavily pregnant with her son, Henry. Michael was a 25-year-old Corporal, born in Limerick, Ireland, then serving with the 12th Dragoons, who had arrived at nearby Hounslow Barracks the previous year. He had attested in London on 14 October 1856 for the Military Train (the forerunner of the Royal Army Service Corps), rising quickly through the ranks to become Troop Sergeant Major before being transferred to the 12th Dragoons five years later, on 1 November 1861. Michael sent me copies of his record, and I read that Michael Connell had a fresh complexion, blue eyes and brown hair, and was a groom when he joined up.

Their first child, Henry, died at the beginning of 1864 when he was less than three months old. Later that year, Elizabeth Ellen became pregnant with a daughter, Margaret Ellen, but on 30 March 1865, while on leave from 12th Dragoons and before Margaret was born, her father Michael Connell died. He died from tuberculosis, although he was not shown as being in hospital at all prior to his going on furlough. Perhaps the army didn't pay much attention to men coughing themselves to death. Sadly, the baby girl also succumbed shortly after birth. Elizabeth Ellen was then just 18 and already a widow with two dead children.

She married again a year later – on 30 May 1866 – this time to 28-year-old Robert Brown, a gunner in the Royal Artillery, son of John Brown, publican, with Sergeant P Connell and Jemima M Smith as witnesses. This was why we hadn't been able to find a marriage between Ellen Dermott and a Mr Brown when we had been looking previously. She was *Elizabeth* Ellen, and her surname at that time was Connell, not Dermott. Michael had obviously been much more diligent than we had been, and had found her straight away. There is no substitute for experience in this game.

We had found the records of her birth and marriages, births of her children and deaths of her husbands, but we hadn't found what happened to Elizabeth Ellen after her two oldest boys entered the workhouse. We tried the 1891 census and the 1901 census with no luck whatsoever. Not only did we not find any record of her, we couldn't find the two youngest children, George and Thomas, either. We figured that, seemingly not one to let the grass grow under her feet, she might have married yet another soldier and disappeared off to parts unknown. We tried the marriage records with no luck. We tried the death records, and there were several possibilities.

Acting on a hunch and remembering it had once cost her £5000 because she had not; Liz invested £7 and sent off for the death certificate of an Elizabeth Ellen Brown who had died in 1886 in Woolwich, Kent, aged 40. She was about the right age, and we knew the family had lived in Woolwich when they were with the Royal Artillery. While we were waiting for the certificate to come, and curious about the £5000, I asked Liz for the story.

The story of the hunch:

Round about 1983, I lived in Worcester and was working with my next door neighbours on a Treasure Hunt organised by the Cadbury chocolate company. They had published a book containing about 10 "stories" each accompanied by a picture. Each story contained clues as to where a treasure worth £5000 (I think it was a golden egg) was buried in different parts of England and Wales.

We had worked out that one of these eggs was buried on the Welsh border and set off one Saturday morning very early to see if we could find it. We came to a small village where we thought it might be and were driving along a small country road when we passed a house with a very distinctive garage (it had 2 doors and was set into a bank at the side of the road.) Now in the top corner of the picture accompanying this "story" was a drawing very similar to it. Unfortunately, we were unable to stop at this point because

98

we were in the middle of road-works so we drove on. No other spot presented itself for a likely place for the buried treasure, so we arrived home empty-handed.

Discussing the matter afterwards, we decided that the only words which might have been a clue to this village was that it was called Main, and there was a sentence in the story which said that a giant hurled a rock "with all his might and main" - and I let my neighbours convince me that this was really too trivial to be of significance - even though there was a building there very similar to one in the picture. Things had to be more complicated than that.

Amongst the instructions for the hunt (which was very highly publicised in the press etc) was one which said that if, for some reason, it was impossible to dig for the treasure in the site selected, competitors should write to Cadbury's with details of where they thought it was and why it could not be dug up. To this day, I cannot begin to imagine why we (I) didn't write and say where we thought our treasure was. At that time, the egg that we were seeking had not been found and it was not even as if we would have ruled ourselves out of the competition by doing so: if we had been wrong, we could have gone on to explore other areas. Anyway, we didn't - and you can imagine how we felt when the results came out and we found that we had been right after all. Just because we had not acted on our hunch we had foregone a treasure!

I've not forgotten that lesson - if there is nothing (or little) to be lost, go for it.

It was obviously a lesson well learned because, ten days later, Liz received the certificate and I got an email which just had *YES!!!!!!!!!!!!!* in the subject line.

Elizabeth Ellen Brown of 8 Cannon Row, Woolwich, widow of Robert Brown, Corporal in the Royal Artillery had *died Suddenly from a Rupture of an Aneurism of the Aorta on 2 May 1886 and it was registered by the Coroner for Kent after an inquest held on 4th May 1886.*

My joy was tinged with a profound sadness that this woman who had become very real to me, seemed to have died, quite literally, from a broken heart.

Buoyed up by her success in finding Elizabeth Ellen's death and getting the confirming certificate, Liz sent away for the death certificate of a Thomas Brown who had died in Lambeth in the second quarter of 1882, the right age for it to be the youngest brother. She got a certificate which said that Thomas (no middle name) Brown died of convulsions on 27 April 1882 in the workhouse infirmary, Brook Street, Lambeth. There was no parent mentioned, and the informant was a Wm Martin, Steward and Inmate of the Workhouse Infirmary.

We needed more information to be able to confirm whether this was or wasn't Elizabeth Ellen's youngest child, Thomas Alfred Brown, and that meant looking up the Lambeth Infirmary records.

I immediately sent a message to Judy in London and she high-tailed it to the National Archives – again. After all, Lambeth was where the family had been living when the grandmother died and when the other children had been sent to Anerley.

Bingo!

He was ours. Judy found the whole family had been admitted to Lambeth workhouse and Thomas had died there.

The whole family was admitted together to the Renfrew Road workhouse on 15 August 1881. Thomas was in and out of the infirmary with his mother until he died in April 1882. The three older boys, Robert, Charles and George, were sent off to the Norwood schools.

The two older boys, Robert James and Charles, went off to Norwood Schools, Elder Road, West Norwood, after two weeks at the Lambeth workhouse and were enrolled there on 30 August

1881. They were aged eleven and five. George was in the infirmary for two weeks, then at the workhouse for another fortnight before being sent off on 16 September, aged three, to join his brothers at school. All three of them were there for nearly a year and were discharged together on 21 July 1882. Robert James and Charles went straight from there to Anerley, where we had already picked up their trail. George Alexander, the youngest surviving child, simply disappeared.

The workhouse records showed that on 10 May 1882, just two weeks after her youngest son Thomas had died, Elizabeth Ellen had been discharged at her own request to a *Mrs Dulwich, 7 Holy Andrew Road, Macauley Road, Clapham.* According to Booth's Poverty Map of London, Macauley Road, Clapham, was in those days an upper-middle to upper class area, so maybe she had gone out 'to service'. After all, she had to make a living. I wanted to think that Elizabeth Ellen, having lost two husbands, two children from her first marriage, three children from her second, and having had to surrender two of her remaining three children to the workhouse, could not bear to lose them all, and kept young George with her after he was discharged from Norwood Schools. She was 35, and he was only four.

Despite not having found out what happened to George, Judy turned up the most amazing piece of information in the form of Elizabeth Ellen's settlement examination. She said she had often wondered why she hadn't been able to find it in the Wandsworth records because there must have been one... after all, the family had been out of the country for seven years, had no support from the military, and the mother would not have been able to get any sort of parish relief without being interviewed as to her circumstances. Knowing now that the family had been admitted to the Lambeth workhouse before the boys had been sent to Anerley, she had searched for it in the Lambeth records and found it there, dated 28 December 1880, just 13 days after Robert had died.

Bless her! She had transcribed the record and sent it to me. It is a poignant document and one I still can't read without being touched and amazed that I am reading my great-grandmother's actual words.

LaBG 140/36
Lambeth Board of Guardians,
Pages 349-350
28 Dec 1880
Ellen Brown
[age] *33*
8 Parade

I am the widow of Robert Brown to whom I was md at Ashford Church Middlesex 30th May 1866 (certificate provided). My husband died at Portsea Hospital 15th December 1880. He was in Royal Artillery, 17th Battery, 9th Brigade. We arrived from India where we have been 7 years. Husband never paid rates. Never apprenticed. He is the son of John and Mary Brown. I never saw his parents and cannot say anything about them. (Copy of attestation produced No. 1655 Robert Brown, Royal Regiment of Artillery, enlisted 12th April 1859 at Dublin, county of Dublin, aged 22 years. Born in the parish of Sth Charlton, town of Alnwick, county of Northampton*. Calling – a Shoeingsmith.) I have four children, Robert James aged 11 years, Charles aged 5 years, Geo Alexander aged 3 years, Thomas Alfred 3 months. I am now living with my mother Elizabeth Dermott. She is having parish relief. My father was in the Army before being Station Master. I do not think he paid rates and never apprenticed. I was born at Wandsworth. I will let you know which part and the date. I will ask Mother.
[additional note] *I Ellen Brown was born in Carters Cottages.*
[clerk's note] *Sent to Wandsworth & Clapham Union*
[* clerk's misreading of Northumberland?]

What a mine of information! We already had, thanks to Michael, the information on where her husband Robert had come

102

from, and from their marriage certificate we had his father's name John, but getting his mother's name Mary, was a real bonus. Because the family had been out of the country for seven years, there had to be a settlement examination to determine which Poor Law Union would have to pay for any support given to Elizabeth Ellen and her children. That was at the source of the questioning that led to answers about Robert's birthplace, parents, whether he or his father had ever been apprenticed or ever paid rates. As it turned out, Elizabeth Ellen's settlement was determined to be in Wandsworth, presumably because she had been born there.

From this document we could see Elizabeth Ellen's connection to the military through her father, and we also (at last) found out why Charles always said he was born in India. His mother had called the West Indies, 'India'. It was years later, while watching an episode of the BBC's *Antiques Roadshow*, that I saw a 19th century geography atlas that showed the 'West India and Bahama Islands', confirming for me that the 20th century's West Indies was originally the (British) West India Islands.

What a lot of work it would have saved us if we had known about this earlier. But that's just the way it goes sometimes.

I found it fascinating to learn my great-grandmother didn't know when or whereabouts in Wandsworth she was born. Things like places and dates of birth were obviously not as important to individuals then as they are now. She also called herself plain Ellen Brown. As she was presumably named for her mother Elizabeth, the family would have called her by her middle name, hence the confusion in the records as to whether she was Elizabeth or Ellen. I just started calling her EE.

After poring over these words I printed them out, put the sheet of paper in an envelope and drove to see my father. Over a cup of coffee at the dining room table I told him I had something very special for him and handed him the envelope. He had never known either set of grandparents – nor had he known any aunts, uncles or cousins. As the youngest and last surviving child of Charles and Sarah, and at 86 years of age, he got a first tangible link to his grandmother. That piece of paper now resides in a tin box along with all his most valuable possessions.

Of course the next thing was to try to find out if we could get the coroner's report of the inquest into EE's death. It might have contained a reference to her having a child with her, and I was quite taken with my assumption that she would have had George with her. I was also interested in getting information about her possible final resting place. Once again I resorted to a begging email. I contacted the North West Kent Family History Society and made contact with a very nice lady called Jan.

I have no idea how she did it or who she had to contact in her search, but one day I got an email from her that just said this:

Elizabeth Ellen Brown's resting place:
Woolwich Old Cemetery,
Kings Highway,
Plumstead SE18
Section F Plot 320

This was fantastic news. Months previously I had decided to go to England as part of an extended overseas trip. Liz had come out to Australia twice and toured with me, and I thought I should repay the compliment. We had arranged to meet in Istanbul, spend 10 days in Turkey, travel to Italy by ferry spending a week in Rome and Sorrento, then fly off to the UK for her to catch up on work she had to do, before setting off to tour the country looking up family records – if we could find any! With this news, Liz and I immediately set in stone a visit to Plumstead.

The next few weeks whizzed by, and nothing more was done before I found myself sitting on a step at Istanbul's airport, waiting for Liz's delayed plane to land. Turkey was a whirlwind of new sights and sounds and a complete break from such concentrated focus on 19th century England. Mind you, with our visits to Troy and Ephesus in Turkey, and to Pompeii and Herculaneum in Italy, we had traveled much further back in the past than the 19th century. A quick flight to London Heathrow and I couldn't wait for the second part of my trip – the one centered on my family.

After having reunited (by email) all the cousins of the Brown family, I had suggested that we have a cousins' reunion while I was in England. Liz had arranged for us to meet up for Sunday lunch at her brother's place. What excitement! One cousin I had never met! Others had not seen each other for 30 years or more! With every ring of the doorbell, a feeling of anticipation swept the room, and the visitor would enter to squeals of delight, hugs and kisses all round. My brother was not able to be there, nor were two of my other male cousins, but we ended up with at least one representative from each family group, and some brought photos and documents which had been handed down from their parents. Not a lot of new information surfaced, except one incomplete family chart drawn up by my Uncle Jim that named a 'George' as a younger brother for Charles. (How I wish I had known that earlier!)

I looked at these people and was amazed that we all had the same grandparents. What a motley crew we were! The two men looked just like all the other Brown men, but the six women really could have been plucked off the street at random: we looked so different. It was a lovely afternoon. We even phoned my father, and each of his nieces and nephews spoke to him and asked him to guess who they were – a bit tough on the old man as he hadn't spoken to a couple of them for almost 60 years.

The next day Liz and I took trains and buses, and braved what was a very cold wind indeed down at docklands, to meet our two researchers, Michael and Judy, who had done such tremendous work for us over the previous months. It was wonderful to meet them in person and to be able to buy them lunch and toast the Browns. Liz and I were off to visit EE's grave at Plumstead after lunch. As it was a bank holiday, Michael, who knew this was on our agenda, had been concerned that we might get to the cemetery to find the office closed and thus not be able to locate the grave. To offset this possibility, he had taken himself off to the cemetery the Thursday before and located the grave (which was unmarked), taken photos (which he gave us), and even told us the route, the bus number, and where to catch it on the way in and way out. We were speechless. He had even found out that our great-grandmother had company in her grave. After she had been lying alone for 50 years, they had buried a young man, 22 years old, on top of her.

Thank goodness Michael had done what he had because, sure enough, not a thing was open. Not even a shop to buy flowers. I couldn't bear the thought of going to the grave without flowers, so I took some that were growing in a low stone wall against the footpath. We lay them as close above her as we could ascertain and spent a few minutes reflecting on her life and times. The flowers would not last. The next mowing would obliterate them and their little note but, as far as we knew, we were the first of her family to stand at her grave for 120 years.

I would count myself very blessed indeed if 120 years after I had died, someone from my family might stand at my grave and remember me.

15. Life in a Northern Town

The town of South Charlton is situated five miles distant from
Alnwick and does one plow day to Alnwick north demesene.
The whole town pays XVIII hens and other bondage services for
repairs of the Castle of Alnwick.

Surveys of 1620 and 1727

The visit to our great-grandmother's grave was the start of a journey through England, in part to visit areas where different streams of my family once lived, and we headed north through Derbyshire to Northumberland, to where we now knew our great-grandfather had been born.

Charles' father Robert Brown, according to his army papers, had been born in South Charlton, a little village near Alnwick in Northumberland. As he was born the year civil registration came into effect and we couldn't find a record of his birth there, we had to look for him in the parish registers of baptisms, marriages and burials. South Charlton, we found, was in the parish of Ellingham, and it was those registers we were after. They are held by the Northumberland Collections Service and are available to view at a place called Woodhorn, near Ashington, a former coal mine. Liz and I earmarked a Sunday to comb the microfilms of the parish records looking for our great-grandfather, and that morning found us sitting in the car park, waiting for the gates to open.

Six hours straight at the records office, and nothing to eat since breakfast except a hot chocolate and a scone, saw both of us exhausted and empty-handed. We had precisely nothing. We had gone there full of high hopes that we would pull the microfilm of the Ellingham parish records off the shelves, look up 1837, and there he would be. Wrong. We had each compiled a bundle of notes taken from the films but we just couldn't find Robert, son of John and Mary Brown. We had resorted to writing down all the Brown baptisms found in the district, and because we hadn't actually exhausted those we determined to return. Having come so far we couldn't bear the thought of going home empty-handed.

In our itinerary we had allowed for an additional day in Northumberland in case we needed it, but we had to wait for two days before we could get back to the records office because they were closed on Mondays and Tuesdays. While we were cooling our heels we took the time to visit South Charlton. It was a nice day for a drive in the country and a chance to do a bit of sightseeing. Despite having travelled extensively in the UK, Liz had not been this far north in England, so it was uncharted waters for both of us. In high spirits, we set off in search of this tiny village.

Coming to a farm that our GPS told us erroneously was South Charlton, we stopped and asked directions to the village, if it was still standing. We told the farmer the story of our great-grandfather who was born there and became a smith before joining the army. The farmer pointed down the road to where a few buildings stood and told us that in the house on the corner opposite the church, lived an old couple, the last of the family of blacksmiths who had been in the village since 1772. We made our way down the hill and parked the car outside the little stone cottage. With a look at each other and a collective deep breath, Liz and I knocked on the door and, despite it being lunch time, were welcomed warmly and asked to come in. It was a good thing that welcome rituals are fairly standardised throughout the western world because we found their Geordie accents very difficult to understand. At the same time, it was fascinating to realise that this was perhaps how our great-grandfather spoke. We spent some time with them, and they were very keen to show us through their property. Their house, Anvil-Croft, was actually on the site of the original chapel that dated from medieval times – it was just two rooms, and the smithy's yard adjoined it.

We discovered that when Robert Brown was born in 1837, the church of St James on the opposite corner to Anvil-Croft had not yet been built, but we visited it anyhow as Liz and I were both quite fond of churches and old graveyards. We were glad we did because we were able to purchase a little booklet there on the Parish of St James and read with interest the history of this place where our ancestor had been born.

Although the village had had a chapel since the 13th century, by the 17th century it was almost in ruins. As far back as 1343, a decree directed the people of South Charlton to contribute to the maintenance of the parish church at Ellingham a few miles away, and the village was also ordered to have two of its inhabitants at Ellingham each Sunday to hear the Vicar's injunctions and to report back to the village. If the South Charlton folk wanted their own local service, they would have to provide the wherewithal themselves. They obviously didn't, because not long after this the chapels at both North and South Charlton fell into ruin.

A 1620 survey listed the village as a market town with *a small number of houses with a town gate or village street which ran directly north on to the open moorland. Unenclosed arable fields were grouped around the village.* By this time, extensive ancient fields had been divided up into smaller ones called Battlefield, Kippetlaw, Gunnerlaw, Chester Hill and Pilerich. I was fascinated to see the military and Scottish elements of those names that are still in use today ('law' meaning a hill). South Charlton apparently had suffered much at the hands of Scottish marauders, and from 1450 Scottish raids had become very regular. As far back as 1538 there was a muster roll that listed four men in the village *able with horse and harness* and 12 men *able without horse and harness.* In the unstable times of the 16th century, these men would no doubt have been called upon to support the Duke of Northumberland.

A 1570 survey listed 17 *tenants at will* and two cottagers, who between them paid a total of £17 18s 9½d in rent to the estate. Ten years later, there were 15 tenants of whom six had weapons. It looked like there was a persistent military presence in this little village. In 1829, each of the inhabitants of the village serving in the Yeoman Cavalry possessed an allotment of 4½ acres with an additional ½ acre in the 'coal ground' between the village and the main road. This land, which was held in return for military service, was called 'bod land', meaning equipment land, presumably because the income it generated provided for the keep and equipment of the Yeomen.

In the mid 19th century the village was demolished and rebuilt on the other side of the main street. We had a look at the bumpy field that was the site of the old village, and took a few photos. There was nothing more the old couple could tell us as they remembered no family by the name of Brown in the village, so we said our goodbyes and left. Driving back we passed through lots of other little villages, all with amazing names – Bolton, Glanton, Wittingham, Callaly, Thropton, Rothbury, Forestburn Gate, Rothley Cross Roads, Cambo, Hartburn and Mitford, then to Longhorsley and Longframlington to Newton-on-the-Moor. The trip through the Northumberland countryside was not only enjoyable but invaluable, as it familiarised me with the place names in the area, and in searches still to be carried out I was able to dismiss some records and look more closely at others I knew to be in the right vicinity.

Despite our best efforts and another six hours amongst the microfilm of the records office two days later, we ended up still not finding Robert. All we had was a bundle of notes – quite a large bundle – and all we could do when we got back home would be to take time to integrate and compare them and hope something would turn up.

Part of the problem was the 1841 census. It was the first of the censuses where names and places of abode had been recorded, and was rudimentary to say the least. Prior to that, the censuses, which started in 1801, were mainly statistical accounts of people in all the settlements of the UK. The 1841 census gave people's names (first and family names but often without any second name), their occupations (sometimes), their gender, and stated whether or not they were born in the same county as they were living, or born in Scotland, Ireland or 'Foreign Parts'. It also gave the place where they were living and their ages. The 1841 census enumerators – the people who copied the individual returns onto the records that we can now view – were instructed to round the ages of people over 15 to the nearest five years, but some rounded them all up and some rounded them all down. Some enumerators, who had to pay for their ink out of their own wages, watered down the ink, making some records so faint they are now impossible to read, while others used pencil, with even poorer results.

Liz and I had already exhausted ourselves looking in the 1841 census for a John and Mary Brown with a three or four-year-old son Robert. No one fitted the bill. Jumping forward to the 1851 census we found some John and Mary Brown couples, but none with a Robert of the right age. We figured perhaps he was off and learning a trade by then because we knew he had turned up in Ireland eight years later in 1859, as a shoeing smith.

Just the day before I was due to fly home to Perth, by following up all the John and Mary Browns we had found from 1841 and 1851 through to 1871, I discovered a John and Mary Ann Brown, who were the closest we could get to being the possible parents of Robert. John Brown was a smith born in Gateshead, Durham, on the south bank of the Tyne, directly across the river from Newcastle. Bearing in mind that on the 1861 census Robert had said he was born in Newcastle-upon-Tyne, I thought this looked promising. John's wife Mary Ann was born in the Alnwick area – again a connection with South Charlton, only five miles away. Perhaps Mary Ann went home to mother to give birth to Robert and returned to the Newcastle area later.

This John and Mary Ann Brown lived in the Byker area of Newcastle-upon-Tyne, and the census showed us that some time between 1861 and 1871, John left smithing and became a publican. As Robert was a smith when he joined the army, and we had it from Robert's marriage certificate in 1866 that his father was a publican, this couple looked like very good candidates to me.

In 1851, John and Mary Ann had three children living with them: all girls – Isabella, aged 11, Ellen, aged 10, and three-year-old Louisa. Back I went to the 1841 census to see if I could pick up a one-year-old Isabella Brown anywhere in the area, but that yielded me nothing either. I tried for all of these children in 1861, but none were living with their parents and I couldn't identify any of them 10 years later on the 1871 census. It was important to follow these girls because, if they were Robert's sisters, their children would be my grandfather's cousins. Liz and I tried marriages and deaths, and while there were some possibilities, I would need to order quite a few certificates if I wanted to eliminate them from my enquiries.

I was stuck. I was off in the morning to catch a plane home, and records that I could have looked at in Northumberland to help me identify this couple were now as far away as the moon.

16. A Mother's Son

I think there must be no heartache like that of losing a child –
for lovers love, childrens love, husbands love, are none of
them so deep and high as mothers love –
it is the highest shape love wears on earth.

Lady Desborough (1867-1952)

Having traced Charles' older bother Robert James as far as we could through both the military records and the censuses, and having discovered the youngest Thomas Alfred had died as a toddler, the only other place we could look for a living relative was via George Alexander. This, after all, was our quest – to find a living relative – or at least to eliminate the possibility of there being one we didn't know about. If George hadn't died in childhood, if he had married, if he had produced children – and if we could find him, then we were in with a chance. A lot of 'ifs' though.

Having found that George had been at Norwood Schools with his two older brothers and was discharged from there on the same day, one would think that he might have been sent either to Anerley with Robert James or to Tooting with Charles. No such luck. He just seemed to have disappeared off the planet. We needed to find out whether he had survived into adulthood, so it was back to the drawing board – or rather the birth, marriage and death indices. That was Liz's department, so she set to work scouring the records – yet again!

Now there were a lot of George Browns in England at the end of the 19th century – and I mean a lot! The surname Brown was, and is, the fourth most common in the UK according to the University College London's spacial literacy program. It is Scottish in origin (Broun), with its home reputed to be in the Dumfries area, with the greatest concentration in Kilmarnock and Galashiels just to the north and east of Dumfries. In 1881 its largest concentrations were between Falkirk in the north and

Northumberland and Durham in the south, and things hadn't changed very much by 1998.

We started with the time that George disappeared from the records – 21 July 1882, when he left Norwood Schools with his two brothers – and we searched and searched. Basically we were looking for his death to try to eliminate him. Searching the censuses for a George Brown who might have said he was born in India, West Indies, Wandsworth (like his brother), or even Lambeth or Norwood, and could have been living anywhere in the UK is just too mammoth a task. If you don't believe me, anyone who would like to try their hand is more than welcome to do so.

No deaths – or at least lots of deaths of George Browns, but none that matched our criteria for age, even within two years.

Chancing our luck with the censuses, because that was all we had, and now knowing that he would have been orphaned with the death of his mother in 1886 when he was eight years old, we found an entry in 1891 for a George Brown about the right age (within a year or so) at the Sutton-at-Hone School for Orphans in Kent – quite near Woolwich. His birthplace was stated as 'London, Middlesex', but we had learned not to put too much store by either stated ages or places of birth.

In desperation, we also earmarked a George Brown on the 1901 census, a railway shunter in Sheerness, Kent – but only because our George's grandfather went into the railways when he left the Army, rising to stationmaster. This George was the right age (23), and his birthplace was, intriguingly, 'not known'.

Well – nothing ventured, nothing gained, so I made some enquiries about the Sutton-at-Hone School for Orphans. From first searches, there didn't seem to be any surviving records until 1897, which was too late for us, but I then enquired further with the North West Kent Family History Society. As usual, I sent an email.

Jan, who had found the whereabouts of Elizabeth Ellen's grave, said she would look into it for me. There was apparently nothing at the Society's library but several other places were put forward as possibly having documents relating to the Sutton-at-Hone

114

orphanage. She enquired at Sutton-at-Hone, Farningham and Dartford libraries, as well as the Medway Archives and Local Studies Centre, the Centre for Kentish Studies and the East Kent Archives Centre but there was pretty much a total lack of information about this orphanage.

Liz had also made enquiries, and eventually we got hold of a place that purported to have the records of the Sutton-at-Hone orphanage, but to get access to George Brown's file we had to make application by way of filling in some forms and demonstrating that we were relatives. The original orphanage was sold off apparently, and the proceeds were donated to the National Children's Home, together with the responsibility for the records. Sutton-at-Hone District School for Orphans (in Huxtable, according to the 1891 census) was really the Swanley Home for Boys at Dartford. Until you get your head around the English system of ecclesiastical parishes, administrative parishes, districts and sub-districts – and if you go back far enough, 'hundreds' – you really don't know what to look under.

We had investigated George as far as this before I went to England, so the scant information about him was packed in the bag ready to produce and try to prove our claim to being the orphan George Brown's relatives. In the end we didn't actually front up, but I made several phone calls, and through either my line of patter or the Australian accent, I managed to get someone there to look up the original records for me. It was from them that I found out that George Brown, aged 14 in 1891, and from London, Middlesex, was actually born in Liverpool. He had been in the school at the same time as a Percy J Brown, also of Middlesex, whom I thought might have been his brother, but I traced Percy back and he was the son of Samuel J Brown, a sailor of Devon and actually had been born in London. I was learning not to trust either ages or birth places and was now much more rigorous in tracking and eliminating people from my search. So it was back to the drawing board in Australia with George.

After some time readjusting to work after being overseas for two months, and just having a rest from the researches, I emailed

Liz and suggested we make a concentrated and systematic effort to locate George. He just didn't disappear into thin air. He must have died at some time, and we had to be able to find him. We needed help here and asked Judy and Michael, both of whom had asked to be updated on the research.

I still clung to my feeling that his mother had taken him with her when the children were discharged from Norwood Schools in July 1882, but I was willing to look at whatever came up. When we first found out what happened to Elizabeth Ellen and that she was the subject of a coroner's inquest, Liz had tried to find out if there was any mention of the event in the local newspapers. She paid a fee to the Greenwich Heritage Centre for a search of the local papers but got a written response that a search of both the *Kentish Independent* and the *Kentish Mercury* for May 1886 had been undertaken and there had been no mention of our great-grandmother. Judy chipped in with the news that there were other local papers around at the time, which might not have been held at the Centre, and she would check them out for us.

What a woman! Back she came just three days later with this:

Woolwich Gazette, 7 May 1886, page 5

Inquest at Woolwich
Mother and Son Parted

An inquest was held at the Castle, Woolwich, on Tuesday evening, on the body of Elizabeth Brown, a widow, who died suddenly at 8 Cannon Row, Woolwich, on Sunday.,

Mrs Berry, deceased's landlady, said that she came home ill on Friday. She got worse and died at 1 a.m. on Saturday.

Mr Watson, surgeon, High-street, said he was called and found life extinct. The post mortem showed disease of the heart and other ailments fully accounting for death.

The body was identified by deceased's son who had been five years at North Surrey schools without having seen his mother. The Jury returned a verdict of "Died from natural causes".

The deceased's infant, two and a half years old, who was found lying by the side of its dead mother, was taken to the workhouse.

The bombshell was in the last sentence. I found myself reading and re-reading this and literally felt my jaw drop. In fact, I just couldn't close my mouth. It was stuck in the open position. I had hoped to find mention of George, who would have been eight, but instead found mention of a totally new child, presumably a boy from the headline, a half-brother to the Browns.

It was a couple of days before Liz and I could gather ourselves, as this hit both of us very hard. There developed an urgency to find out about this little one. What was his name and what happened to him? I was haunted by the image of this child lying beside his cold, dead mother and then being carted off and dumped in a workhouse. Judy, in the meantime, had quietly taken herself off and looked up the records of the nearest workhouse, Plumstead, and found him admitted there on 3 May 1886. His name was William Thomas. He was in the workhouse from May to September, then he was admitted to the Woolwich Union Infirmary, where he languished for two years until he died on 22 February 1888, aged five. I burst into tears. Another dead child.

It turned out that the poor mite had been born in a workhouse and died in one. His mother had admitted herself to the Woolwich Infirmary on 4 September 1883 from 32 Beresford Rd, Woolwich and gave birth the same day. Both mother and child were discharged on 19 July the next year, not from the workhouse but from the infirmary, so it appeared that there was some problem either with EE or the baby. Liz ordered William's death certificate and it stated he died of 'hydrocephalic convulsion'. That must have meant that the baby had water on the brain and was probably why he spent so much time in the infirmary. No wonder Elizabeth

Ellen had 'heart' disease: all of her children had been lost to her before they turned 12.

There was one other piece of information in Judy's email. She had also gone back to the records for Anerley and found there a reference to our two Brown boys:

North Surrey School District
Minutes of the Board of Management
Meeting of 17 May 1886, at Anerley

" ... The Superintendent [of the schools] *reported ... that at the request of the Coroner he had sent two boys named Brown to identify the body of their Mother who had died suddenly at Woolwich, and subsequently to attend the funeral & that he had paid their traveling expenses & those of the Porter who took charge of them. The Board resolved that the course taken by the Superintendent be approved."*

So this was where Charles got his memory of seeing his dead mother laid out – not on board ship but in the Woolwich morgue. He was just 10 years old. Forty-five years later when his own daughter died he prevented my father, then also 10 years old, from going to her funeral. All his life, he insisted that funerals weren't the place for children. And from his experience, they weren't. This new knowledge made me doubly thankful I had had the opportunity to stand in his steps at his mother's grave and mark her life.

And we were still left with George! He wasn't with his mother when she died and hadn't been called upon by the Coroner, so where was he? EE must have told the people she was either living or working with, that she had two sons in Anerley, otherwise the Coroner would not have known. The most likely person was her landlady, Mrs Berry, who had given evidence at the inquest. I checked the Berry family on the 1881, 1891 and 1901 censuses and found out that she had a large and seemingly close family, its

118

members living very near each other in Woolwich over a period of at least 20 years, but I could find no trace of a George anywhere who might have been EE's son and been taken in by the family. Something must have happened to him – either he died or was sent to a different institution from his two brothers, or maybe overseas, perhaps to Canada. I favoured his death because I couldn't believe he would not have been mentioned by his mother if he had been alive, no matter where he was.

I had gone through all the George Browns who died between 1882 when the three boys left Norwood Schools, and 1886 when their mother died. There was no George Brown death in the whole of England that matched the age – even approximately – of our George. The fact that his mother had been admitted to the Woolwich Infirmary to have William, and spent nearly a year there, must mean that George was either dead or somewhere else, because he would have been less than six years old and yet was not admitted with her. That narrowed the search gap even more, to a period of just over a year between 21 July 1882 and 5 September 1883. And search we did. Judy covered all the Woolwich institutions for that period, plus the Lambeth workhouse at Renfrew Road where they had first been admitted, in case George had been sent back there after being at Norwood Schools. Nothing. She backtracked to St James School, Tooting, where Charles had been sent before he went to Anerley, looking for the admission of a George Brown. She found one George Brown there who had been discharged to St Mary's Roman Catholic Orphanage and from there fostered out a couple of times before being consigned to the training ship *Exmouth,* and from there apprenticed to a tailor. By 1901 he was a 'Chemist Porter'. This George was two years younger than our George, and a Catholic, so we didn't think it was him. Two years might not make a lot of difference in an adult but George was only four when he left Norwood Schools and there is a lot of difference between a four year old and a two year old.

Liz had also been delving and found a George Brown of the right age on the 1891 census, working as a waiter at the Bald-Faced Stag at Chigwell (Essex) and whose birthplace was given as

Penge. We were really scratching the bottom of the barrel. Penge was where Anerley House was but we had no evidence at all that George had gone there. Nevertheless, we were not a family to let any stone go unturned. Liz tried to find him on the 1881 census but her search was inconclusive. She then went forward to 1901 and looked for a Penge-born George Brown. Only one came up, a labourer, now married to Eliza and living in West Ham. She thought this one must be the same one she'd found 10 years earlier, and Judy thought he might have married Eliza Cass in June 1899. Liz decided to order that marriage certificate to see if a Robert Brown was cited as George's father. It was a very long shot because not even Charles, George's older brother, got his father's name right on his marriage certificate. No, this George's father's name was William, which set Liz on another search to see if she could locate a George, son of William, on the 1881 census. No go there, but she did find a William Brown living very close by, who could have been George's brother for he was born in Anerley, Surrey, and we know Anerley is in Penge. That sent Liz off delving into the spreadsheets we had created of the Browns at Anerley House to see if she could find brothers George and William Brown to possibly eliminate them from our investigations. No go there, either. I had gone through them all with millimetric precision. Not being able to either rule this George in or rule him out, we left him in the 'pending' basket.

All in all, with suggestions from Liz and me, Judy had searched the creed registers, school records and Board of Guardians records for: Westminster, Lambeth and Wandsworth & Clapham Unions; South Metropolitan and North Surrey School Districts; Lambeth and Woolwich workhouses and infirmaries – with a singular lack of success. She had also gone through their registers of deaths and apprenticeships. We had all searched the civil death indices. No go at all.

By this time, if you have been trying to follow all this your head must be spinning, and you will be experiencing what most family historians experience at some time or another as they bash their heads up against yet another brick wall. Unless Michael could find him, we would have to assume that George had been abducted by aliens.

17. Who's Who?

In England and Wales, the most popular female and
male names given to babies born in 1800 were Mary
and John, with 24% of female babies and 22% of male
babies receiving those names, respectively.

Douglas Galbi 'Long-TermTrends in Personal
Given Name Frequencies in the UK', 2002

It was quite a while after I had returned from England – about a year in fact – that I began again my search for John and Mary Brown. My travels there had given me a familiarity with the area that I would never otherwise have had and I tackled it with some confidence. I wanted to sort out the children of this John and Mary Ann Brown I had found. Isabella had been born in Gateshead, Durham, the same as her father; Ellen, just a year younger, had been born in Deptford, Kent; and the baby, Louisa, in Newcastle-upon-Tyne, Northumberland, where the family was living in 1851.

Name	Mary Ann ...
Birth	~1807 Alnwick, Northumberland
Husband	John BROWN, smith / publican b. Gateshead, Durham
Children	Isabella b ~1840 Gateshead, Durham
	Ellen b ~1841 Deptford, Greenwich, Kent
	Louisa b ~1849 Newcastle

I couldn't figure out why the middle child would have been born south of the Thames, 460km (285 miles) away, when the other two were born either side of the Tyne. The only thing I could think of was that both places were centres of shipbuilding, and Deptford also had a military depot. Perhaps John Brown was or had been a smith with the army? I just had to find out.

The first step seemed to be to get the birth certificate of one of these children to check the mother's maiden name, father's occupation and place of abode when the child was born.

I sent away for birth certificates for two Isabella Browns who were born in the 4th quarter of 1840 in Gateshead. They were the only two of the right age, but neither of their parents were John and Mary Ann. Fortunately, I had ordered the certificates using the parents' names as checking criteria, and as they didn't match the names of the parents of these two Isabellas, no certificates were produced and it cost me only the search fee. As there were no other Isabellas born around that time in Gateshead, I had to give up on her.

For the second daughter, I had found an Ellen Brown born in Deptford in the 3rd quarter of 1841, and I found on the internet that there were some people who had access to the Deptford registers and were willing to do limited lookups. So I sent an email. The information I got back was confusing to say the least. The Ellen Brown born in Deptford was the daughter of a John George Brown and Mary Ann Teer, who married in 1838 at Lewisham, Kent. Hmmm, John and Mary Ann – the names matched, but if they were the couple I was looking for, why would they have been married in Kent when both of them came from the north of England? They also had two other girls – Elizabeth in 1839 and Mary Ann in 1843 – both born in the registration district of Greenwich, which includes Deptford.

Surely this must be a different family, otherwise these girls would presumably show up living with their parents in Newcastle in 1851. I tried but couldn't find another John and Mary Ann Brown with matching children on the 1841 or 1851 census. The other two children could have died of course, and records show that there were at least six Elizabeths and one Mary Ann Brown, who died in Greenwich between 1841 and 1849.

Name	Mary Ann TEER
Marriage	Q3 1838, Lewisham, Kent
Husband	John George BROWN
Children	Elizabeth b 2Q 1839, Greenwich, Kent
	Ellen b Q3 1841, Greenwich, Kent
	Mary Ann b Q1 1843 Greenwich, Kent

John Brown and Mary Ann Teer married in 1838, so if Robert was part of their family, he would either have been an illegitimate child or Mary Ann could have been a widow, which could account for my not being able to find Robert's baptism in the parish registers under the name Brown. But if this couple (whose children Elizabeth, Ellen and Mary Ann were born in Deptford) was the same couple who were living in Newcastle in 1841 with their children Isabella (born in Durham), Ellen (born in Kent) and Louisa (born in Northumberland), what were they doing ploughing up and down the country from year to year? If they were the same couple, they would have had to have been in Northumberland in 1837, Kent in 1838, up in Durham in 1840, back in Kent in 1841 and back in Northumberland in 1849. Surely only the army would have moved them that much.

Another problem was that the Mary Ann I was looking for was supposedly born in Alnwick, but I found no Mary Ann Teer born in Alnwick. Of course I only had the word of the person who did the looking up in the Deptford records that this couple were the parents of these children, but because I didn't have access to the records myself, I had to take that on trust.

I sent for the birth certificate of a Louisa Brown, born in Newcastle in the 4th quarter of 1848, and kept my fingers crossed that this would reveal that her parents were also John and Mary Ann Brown and would show both the occupation of the father and the maiden name of the mother. Well it did all right – her father was John Brown, a smith, and her mother was Mary Ann... Kennedy. Not Teer. Oh dear!

Name	Mary Ann KENNEDY	Mary Ann TEER
Birth	~1807 Alnwick, Northumberland	
Marriage	Q4 1842 Stepney, London	Q3 1838, Lewisham, Kent
Husband	John BROWN, smith / publican b. Gateshead, Durham	John George BROWN
Children	Isabella b ~1840 Gateshead, Durham	Elizabeth b 2Q 1839, Greenwich, Kent
	Ellen b ~1841 Deptford, Greenwich, Kent	Ellen b Q3 1841, Greenwich, Kent
	Louisa b ~1849 Newcastle	Mary Ann b Q1 1843 Greenwich, Kent

I checked out the marriage of Mary Ann Kennedy to John Brown and found that it was at the end of 1842 – after both Isabella and Ellen were born! Did I have a second marriage here? I had no idea.

Well, at least I did know now that we had two families, despite some confusion around their children and place of abode. Where to from here? In an effort to bring some order into this confusion, I thought I would sort out all the paperwork, which somehow just piles up in disheveled heaps around my computer, leaving me just enough room for the keyboard. In going through all the bits of paper, I came across the previously sent-for death certificate of a Mary Ann Brown, who had died in Byker, Newcastle-upon-Tyne, who I thought at the time might have been the wife of John Brown, the smith-turned-publican.

Death certificates give the address of the deceased at the time of death and the name and address of the informant. I had thought that it might give the name of her husband and where he was living at the time of her death – or even name a pub, if I was lucky, but it had proved to be a disappointment. The husband (then dead), although a John Brown, was a chair maker not a publican, and I had discounted it. As I looked at it again, I thought that 'chair maker' was a strange occupation. Surely anyone who made chairs would make other furniture as well and would be either a furniture maker or joiner. Inspecting it closely and under the magnifying glass, I realised that it was not chair maker but chain maker! Making chain was the job of a smith, and there were whole towns devoted to that occupation. In the shipbuilding industry, there were a myriad of chains that needed to be made, not the least of which was an anchor chain. What a dope I was! Another example of what having expectations can do for you. Once I saw that this Mary Ann was the widow of John Brown, I expected his occupation to be 'publican' and when I didn't see that, I just disregarded the certificate as being for some other Mary Ann Brown.

Looking with much more interest now, I saw the informant was her son-in-law, Frederick William McGregor, and that she was living with him when she died. A son-in-law means a daughter, and if I found him, I might find her daughter. Would she be an Elizabeth, an Isabella, an Ellen, a Mary Ann or a Louisa... or, heaven help me, someone else?

I could not find a birth registration for Frederick William McGregor or any other mention of him prior to 1881, but on the 1881 census there was a Frederick W McGregor, born in 1843 in Newcastle-upon-Tyne, a waterman, and his wife, Mary Ann, born in London in 1843. They were still living in Byker, an area of Newcastle, and they had two children.

Mary Ann! Was she the daughter of the Deptford couple, or was she a daughter of the Northumberland couple and living elsewhere at the time of the 1851 census? Or were those two couples the same? And if so, was Louisa, whose birth certificate I had, the daughter of yet another John and Mary Ann? It was all getting too, too confusing.

Name	Mary Ann KENNEDY	Mary Ann TEER	Mary Ann ----
Birth	~1807 Alnwick, Northumberland		~1807
Marriage	Q4 1842 Stepney, London	Q3 1838, Lewisham, Kent	
Husband	John BROWN, smith / publican b. Gateshead, Durham	John George BROWN	John BROWN, 'chain maker' (smith)
Children	Isabella b ~1840 Gateshead, Durham	Elizabeth b 2Q 1839, Greenwich, Kent	
	Ellen b ~1841 Deptford, Greenwich, Kent	Ellen b Q3 1841, Greenwich, Kent	
	Louisa b ~1849 Newcastle	Mary Ann b Q1 1843 Greenwich, Kent	Mary Ann b ~1843, London (living Byker, Newcastle) m. Q1 1870 Frederick William McGREGOR (waterman) b Newcastle

I wrote to Liz:

I'm confused and I have spent all day on this! I have potentially three Mary Ann Browns (wife of John Brown) –
i) Mary Ann Kennedy whose husband was John Brown the smith who was the mother of Louisa (and Isabella and Ellen?)
ii) Mary Ann Brown who died in Byker in 1876 who was the widow of the "chain maker" and the mother of Mary Ann born in London.

*iii) Mary Ann Teer who gave birth to Elizabeth, Ellen &
Mary Ann in Greenwich.
This reminds me of my 1, 2 or 3 Charles Browns!*

She could add nothing to this, so, tired, irritated and vaguely depressed, I set John and Mary Ann Brown aside for a while.

Strangely, boredom came to my rescue.

I was doing a stint as a volunteer at the genealogical society's library and, it being rather quiet on a Monday night, I started mooching around in some of the large files I had noticed but hadn't looked at. In some of them were lists of specific microfiche held by the library pertaining to the various counties of England. I flicked through to Northumberland and saw that they had Northumberland marriages between 1813 and 1837. This was a period of time I was very interested in – the years leading up to Robert Brown's birth and the presumed marriage of his mother and father. I checked the microfiche and there were 11 John Browns who married either a Mary or a Mary Ann. Two of those marriages were in the Alnwick area, and Alnwick was only about five miles from South Charlton, where Robert was born. The most interesting by far was the marriage on 12 May 1836 (the year before Robert was born) of John Brown to Mary Nicholson. I jumped at that name! Robert Brown's second son was baptised John Nicholson. Such an unusual middle name might easily be his mother's maiden name. I knew that it was quite common for one child to be named in such a way, even in modern times. The brother of an old boyfriend of mine carried his mother's maiden name as a middle name. What was more, this was the marriage of a John and Mary, not a John and Mary Ann, so could well be the couple I was looking for. I decided to pursue this tack and put aside the confusing John and Mary Ann scenario.

I immediately looked up the Mormons' International Genealogical Index records to see if I could get any information on Mary Nicholson, and found out she was the daughter of John Nicholson, joiner, and his wife Mary Thew, and that she was baptised in the parish of Ellingham on 16 March 1812. This was surely Robert's mother! South Charlton was in the parish of Ellingham.

I rushed off and ordered some microfilm from the family history centre of the local Mormon Church, determined to follow up this new information. I ordered microfilms of baptisms, deaths and marriages for both the Alnwick and Ellingham areas – Alnwick because that was where Mary Nicholson had married, and Ellingham because I wanted to go through those records with a fine-tooth comb to see if I could find anything that Liz and I might have missed when we went through them in Northumberland.

Films ordered from the Mormons can take between three weeks and several months to arrive, so in the meantime I decided to chart all of the Nicholsons and Browns living in the Alnwick and Ellingham registration districts at the time of the 1841 census. Relationships weren't recorded in 1841 but at least I would have family groups and where they were living in relation to each other. I found out that very few Nicholsons were living in Alnwick and very few Browns were living in Ellingham.

In South Charlton there were what looked like three family groups. I found who I was sure were Mary Nicholson's parents, although I couldn't find Mary herself under either Nicholson or Brown. I did however find a Robert Nicholson the same age as Robert Brown would have been, living with Mary's parents, John and Mary Nicholson. With them were a daughter and four children who were definitely not theirs but could well have been their grandchildren or at least of that generation. I would just have to wait for the films to come to sort out who was who. Maybe John and Mary Brown's marriage record, if I found it, would throw some light on the situation.

Nicholsons in South Charlton – 1841 Census

John	**Nicholson**	60	joiner
Mary	Nicholson	55	
Martha	Nicholson	25	
Michael	Nicholson	7	
John	Nicholson	6	
Robert	Nicholson	4	
Mary	Nicholson	2	
William	**Nicholson**	53	cartwright
Eleanor	Nicholson	22	
Isabella	Nicholson	20	
Mary	Nicholson	16	
John	Nicholson	14	
James	Nicholson	10	
Michael	Nicholson	12	
Robert	**Nicholson**	50	cartwright
Jane	Nicholson	42	

Of all the Browns living in Alnwick in 1841, there were only seven Johns. Four were in families (two were the heads of families and two were children under 10), so I knew I could discount them. The other three John Browns were living on their own. One was a 14-year-old boy (too young), one a 60-year-old man (too old), and the other a blacksmith, whose age was recorded as 35 (but who could have been any age between 35 and 39 because of the rounding). He had been born in Scotland. I thought he might be a possibility, but he was living in lodgings in Queens Head Yard and there was no sign of a woman with him. I didn't even know if he was single or married. You had to find an individual 10 years later on the 1851 census to get an exact age and their marital status.

I tried to locate this John Brown, blacksmith, on the 1851 census but couldn't. He could have died, moved on or gone back to Scotland. John and Mary weren't exactly unusual names. No, I just had to wait for the microfilms to come.

And come they did. The Alnwick ones first. I pounced on them and after three or four four-hour sessions transcribing the baptisms and marriages (and some deaths) of all the Browns and Nicholsons I could find on two reels of microfilm, I spent uncounted hours typing them all into spreadsheets and trying to match them up. I had deaths from 1728 to 1822, marriages from 1647 to 1869 and baptisms from 1700 to 1849. Did I finally have something concrete that would lead me forward?

My major find was the marriage certificate of John Brown and Mary Nicholson, which stated they were bachelor and spinster both of Alnwick parish (although I knew Mary was a native of Ellingham parish, so she must have been working in Alnwick); they married after banns and *with the consent of parents*. At first reading, this seemed to indicate that one of them was underage, which is normally stated if that is the case, but Mary would have been 23. I asked around but no one seemed to know what this phrase really meant and further investigation suggested it might mean that it was the witnesses who were consenting. Other entries in the marriage register said *with the consent of friends* and it seemed that witnesses to those marriages could indeed be friends and not family, as they didn't have the same surnames as the bride and groom. The witnesses for John and Mary's marriage were John Nicholson (her father?), Ann Nicholson (she had a sister, Ann), and a Joseph Robertson, whom I figured might have been a mate of the groom.

In the baptism records, I found a dozen John Browns between 1716 and 1848 and I could obviously eliminate most of them as being born either too early or too late. As Mary was born in 1812, I was looking for someone born between, say, 1800 and 1815, which would have made him between 21 and 36 when they married. There was just one – John Brown, born in 1801 to a farmer, Thomas Brown of Alnham, and his wife, Margaret Scott, of South Charlton! Hey hey… was this him? There were 10 other children in that family and they all were born either in Alnham or at a place called White House Folly in Abbey Lands, only a spit from South Charlton in the district of Alnwick. I scurried back to the family history centre to order more microfilms, this time for Alnham parish.

In the meantime (I'm not a very patient person) I would see if I could track this family of Browns on the censuses. I searched for all of Thomas and Margaret Brown's progeny on the 1841 and 1851 censuses. It seemed that while John's parents and married sisters stayed in either Alnwick, North Charlton or Abbey Lands, his brothers moved down to Shotley Bridge in Durham. I found a John Brown, who was most likely the John Brown (son of Thomas and Margaret) that I was looking for, married not to Mary Nicholson but to Ann Moore, mother of their nine children (none of them a Robert).

Following this John in 1841 and 1851, I found he was a labourer in Longbenton in 1841 and a coal miner in Medomsly (which is only 2 miles from Shotley Bridge) in 1851. I was pretty sure he was the John Brown who was Thomas and Margaret's son, but the killer blow came when I checked him out on the 1861 census, where he was a 'farmer of 100 acres employing two men and one boy' in Lanchester, Durham, and his birthplace was stated as 'White House Folly'. That clinched it for me. This was not the John Brown that Mary Nicholson had married. I let Liz know and settled down to wait for the Ellingham records. Once they arrived, I would once again have my work cut out for me. And arrive they did.

It was back to the microfilm reader for hours and hours at a time, but Ellingham is much smaller than Alnwick and this time there was only about three-quarters of one film to go through. I used the same methodology as before, transcribing all the Brown and Nicholson entries in pencil then, at home, entering them onto spreadsheets and sorting them into family groups in a rough time line. As I write this, I am amazed I can dismiss so much work in just one sentence.

My objective was to identify relatives for this Robert Nicholson, aged four, whom I had found on the 1841 census, and it was only after going through the Ellingham parish records for Nicholson baptisms, marriages and deaths that I would be able to establish any relationships between the family groups.

What I discovered was that the family group with whom Robert Nicholson was living in South Charlton in 1841 consisted of his grandparents (as I had suspected), who were John and Mary (Thew) Nicholson; their daughter, Martha Nicholson, who never married; his two cousins, Michael and Mary Ann Nicholson, who were the illegitimate children of Martha's sister, Eleanor; and John Nicholson, the illegitimate son of Mary Nicholson, who was by then married to John Brown. Yes, that bit was a surprise – not that there were illegitimate children in the family, that was quite common, but if this young Robert was indeed Robert Brown (despite being recorded as a Nicholson), he had a half-brother called John Nicholson. Our Robert Brown had called his second son by that very same name! I couldn't see how this was not the family we had been looking for.

Nicholsons of South Charlton (Ellingham District) – 1841 Census

John	Nicholson	60	son of William and Eleanor
Mary	Nicholson	55	wife of John
Martha	Nicholson	25	unmarried daughter of John & Mary
Michael	Nicholson	7	son of Eleanor, grandson of John & Mary
John	Nicholson	6	son of Mary, grandson of John & Mary
Robert	Nicholson	4	? son of Mary & John Brown, grandson of John & Mary
Mary Ann	Nicholson	2	daughter of Eleanor, granddaughter of John & Mary

By following the registers and the censuses, I was able to account for every one of the children and grandchildren of John Nicholson and his wife Mary Thew, and the only one that I couldn't attribute to any of the Nicholsons was Robert – unless he was actually Robert Brown. He only fitted if he was Robert Brown. I also tracked all the children and grandchildren of John's brother William Nicholson, who also had a number of his extended family living with him, too. Robert did not fit in there either.

I figured that this Robert Nicholson had to be our Robert Brown and that in 1841 he had just been given the same surname as everyone else in the family group. I found the same thing had happened in 1871 when Andrew and Thomas Scott, sons of William Nicholson's widowed daughter Mary Scott, were living with their uncle John Nicholson. They too were recorded on that census as Nicholson, instead of Scott.

Lots of members of this family at one time or another stayed with their siblings, uncles or grandparents. As the years rolled on, cousins and maiden aunts went to live with other members of the family once their own parents had died. I tracked them all up to 1901 – just in case I ran across a Robert Nicholson born in 1837 who suddenly popped up in one of the censuses, but none did. No matter how hard I looked though, I couldn't find his mother Mary – nor could I find Mary's two closest sisters, Eleanor and Ann Nicholson.

All the Nicholson men married, but the women were a bit more... unconventional. Of John and Mary's daughters:

- Martha never married and lived with her parents until they died, then moved in with first her sister Ann, then when she died, moved in with sister Elizabeth;
- Eleanor had two children as a single woman (one when she was 24 the other four years later) and both, sadly, died in childhood;
- Mary had a son John before marrying John Brown. John Nicholson was raised by his grandparents, married and had children and grandchildren;
- Ann married later in life (although not as late as her husband thought, as she was born in 1814 but by 1861 she said she was born in 1827, having dropped 13 years), and she died some time between 1871 and 1881;
- Jane married in 1854 and died some time between 1891 and 1901 without having had any children that I could find; and
- Elizabeth married a widower from Yorkshire in 1862 and also had no children.

Of the daughters of John's brother William:

- Eleanor didn't marry and disappeared after the 1841 census leaving an illegitimate daughter Mary Jane, who went on to marry and have children of her own and always lived with (or next door to) her mother's brother John;
- Isabella never married but had a son Robert who died in 1853 aged six; and
- Mary married and had two sons (and, unusually for this family, in that order) but was widowed young. She and her two sons lived with her brother John before she died some time between 1861 and 1871.

All very interesting, but none of that really brought us any closer to John Brown's ancestry. I said to Liz that I might have to keep ordering registers until I have covered all of Northumberland (oh no!) and found all the John Browns that were born in that county between 1800 and 1815... and, anyway, John could have been born in Scotland! Finding Robert's mother had turned out to be a mammoth undertaking and I had no more energy for searching further. It seemed to be a natural full stop, so that's what I did – I rested for a while.

18. One Door Closes

When one door closes, another opens; but we often look so long and so regretfully upon the closed door that we do not see the one which has opened for us.

Alexander Graham Bell (1847-1922)

I eventually resumed a normal level of genealogical activity, finding that this resting is a very necessary part of research. No one can go on and on at a frenetic pace, because there needs to be a process whereby energy levels are topped up, and time given to the inner recesses of the brain to make connections that the conscious mind can't make on demand. It's a time of consolidation and getting the paperwork in some semblance of order, although trying to get an adequate filing system for genealogical research has not been successfully achieved by anyone – not to my knowledge. It's a good thing really that I had an academic background in anthropology, for it had prepared me in some way for the extent of the tentacles of this sort of research. In fact, when I look back on it, I had always found myself (often reluctantly) embroiled in kinship systems in my undergraduate study. Regardless of how I started out, I always seemed to end up in kinship systems. I was offered further study in this area but family commitments prevented me from being able to take up the offer. I regretted it for a long time until I realised that my studies were simply the preparation I needed for the work I was now doing – finding families.

Always on the search for possible sources of information, I had attended a seminar at the genealogical society on what gems could be found in their library, and upon my return home I decided to check on some Dowding family details – just to tie up a few loose ends. I opened *ancestry.com* and typed in the name Frederick James Dowding, his place and year of birth. While waiting for the screen to load, I quickly sent a couple of emails. One of these was to Liz and Judy proposing to close the door on George Alexander

Brown, at least for the time being, because all of us had exhausted all the avenues we could think of. Closing down my email program, I returned to the *ancestry.com* screen and there, at the top of the list, was a military record for 1895 for Frederick J Dowding, born St Olives (read St Olaves). I knew that St Olaves was the parish of Bermondsey in Surrey where most of the Dowding children had been born, so I clicked the link and what opened was the first of seven pages of records that confirmed that this indeed was Charles' brother-in-law. I was gobsmacked! I believe that when one door closes another one opens, but I couldn't say I had ever witnessed it happening so fast.

I never knew when the Dowding family had returned to England, and I certainly never knew Frederick James had gone into the army! This was quite a find and I quickly printed off his record. He attested for the Cheshire Regiment on 20 March 1895. That gave me an approximate time that the rest of the family might have returned to England from America. I knew they were back in England before 1900 because my grandfather had been dating my grandmother at that time (more information that had come from my father in a roundabout way). Dad said his mother had told him that someone had run into a theatre where she and Charles were watching a show, and shouted out the news that the 217-day siege of 1200 British soldiers at Mafeking, begun just two days after the outbreak of the Boer War, was over. That would have been on 18 May 1900 – or 17 May if they had been in Twickenham, which for some unknown reason got the news one day before it was officially announced.

The last page of Fred Dowding's military record was his military history sheet and against *Name and Address of Next of Kin* was the information that confirmed the family's return. Next of kin was his father, Frederick Dowding, of 60 High Street, Walthamstow, Essex, which had been crossed out and replaced with *Park Road, Bushey Nr Watford, Herts*. This confirmed that the family had returned before Fred joined the army, i.e. prior to March 1895. I don't know what they were doing in Walthamstow, or when they moved, but by the time of the 1901 census the family was living in Bushey.

I found out from these documents that when blue-eyed, dark-haired, 20-year-old Fred joined up, he was a woollen spinner, a skill no doubt gained from working in the mills in Connecticut. He was just 5ft 4⅛in tall (1.63m) and 132lb in weight (less than 60kg). I knew all the Dowding women were short – so were the men apparently. He had scars on his chin and right groin and he was a Baptist. That was something else confirmed. My father's family was non-conformist and that must have come through from the Dowding side. One of Dad's brothers was a London City Missionary, and two of his sisters were quite strict —the family attending the Plymouth Brethren church and local Quaker meeting house.

Fred had joined up in Aldershot and was granted good conduct pay of one penny a day on the second anniversary of his attestation, so he seemed to be a man of disciplined habits – rather unlike the army men from the Brown side of the family. After another four years, he was granted two pence a day good conduct pay – again on his anniversary. He initially signed up for what was termed a Short Service, which was seven years with the Colours (meaning on active service), and five years in the Reserve, or, if the man completed his seven years' service while overseas, then for eight years with the Colours and four years in the Reserve. In 1901 while in India, he extended his service to complete 12 years with the Colours under provisions that allowed for *a bounty of £150 and a gratuity of £247.80 in lieu of furlough to England,* and served seven years in India from 28 October 1897 to 11 November 1904. He didn't return to England during his overseas service, so pocketed the bounty and the gratuity.

While in India he was appointed a bandsman, but reverted to private at his own request – after he had returned to England, and a year before he was discharged on 19 March 1907. He married local girl Lizzie Fowler straightaway, and when he signed on with the Yorkshire Regiment in July of that year, to serve out his four years in the Reserves, he was a chauffeur, living with Lizzie in nearby Tamworth.

Four years later, according to the 1911 census, Fred was working as a chauffeur and had moved to 35 Shakespeare Street, Watford, where his mother's family, the Barnetts, came from. He died on 13 October 1934 of carcinoma of the esophagus, so I wonder if he was a smoker, although alcohol will do that for you too.

Now knowing that my father had this real Uncle Fred who had spent seven years in India (and quite probably caught malaria – and possibly other diseases!), my thoughts turned to the man Dad knew as Uncle Fred, whom his mother and a neighbour had nursed. Was this indeed Sarah's brother, and could I stop speculating that it was Charles' brother who had syphilis and who had been to India and caught malaria there? As my Uncle Jim had thought his father's brother (Robert James) was called Frederick, I had entertained the thought that he might have been called Fred as a nickname. But here was another, more likely scenario – that Uncle Fred was indeed Uncle Fred Dowding. Certainly Fred J Dowding was short – he was 5ft 4in, having lost an eighth of an inch by the time he was 32 (the army was ever precise), and he was certainly likely to have lost more height as he aged. At the time that he may have been living with his sister's family he would have been going on for 55, and he died before he turned 60. As his wife was still alive at the time my father remembers Uncle Fred (she was the informant on his death certificate), I wondered what he would have been doing living away from her and being nursed by someone else? Or perhaps the 'neighbour' was really his wife Lizzie, and as they had no children, maybe they had called on his sister for help when Fred got sick. I have come to believe that this is the true story of Uncle Fred and possibly some of the 'facts' of my father's story may have got twisted over the years – as had Charles' story of his own origins.

Being thrilled at finding one end of this tangled ball of string we call family history, I sent an email to Michael, cheekily informing him that he wasn't the only one who could find dead soldiers.

19. Wild Geese

The term 'Wild Geese' is used in Irish history to refer to Irish soldiers in British and European armies from the 16th century. It was estimated that by 1860 some two thirds of the British Army, including the English county regiments, was constituted of Irishmen or their descendants.

Various

At the same time as we were conversing about Fred Dowding, I asked Michael if he would check up on James Dermott, Elizabeth Ellen's father, who had been in the army before being a railway stationmaster. I had looked up some records and found out there were at least two regiments stationed in Guernsey in 1801 when James was born, so I figured there was a strong possibility he himself might have been the son of a soldier. I thought there was no point in not checking out everyone, as the army kept cropping up in my family.

As always, Mike was on it like a shot.

We are leaving for the airport in 40 minutes. Just received your e-mail and have just done a quick search on the TNA catalogue for James Dermott. Only one comes up in WO97 soldiers discharged to pension 1760-1854.

James Dermott born Colchester, Essex, served in the 6th Dragoons between 1815-1843 and discharged 1843 age 42.

I had to smile. Here he was, about to jump in a taxi for the airport and he is looking up the National Archives catalogue for my great-great-grandfather. And what's more, he was spot on!

I spent some time checking out the 6th Dragoons – quite a posh regiment with a decorated history. The 6th Dragoons operated initially out of Enniskillen Castle, Ireland, but after 1756 they spent several generations away from Ireland and the regiment's name evolved to the 'Inniskillings'. Some of the regiment went to

America in 1812, and they fought at Waterloo in early 1815 (not our James Dermott though, because he joined up later that year), and much later they were part of the charge of the Heavy Brigade at Balaklava during the Crimean War.

Michael found out that:

There were five infantry regiments in Guernsey in 1802 plus companies of the RA and RE as well as a couple of militia regiments. James of the Dragoons, attested at the age of 14 on 10th August 1815 in London and was tailor by trade. James was discharged to pension on 10th October 1843 and shows his intended place of residence to be London in the County of Middlesex.

The pension registers record that James was receiving his pension first in South London. In 1865 he is then shown receiving it in the Taunton district where he continues to receive it until 1871. This does not mean he was living in Taunton, only that this was probably the closest to where he was living. We know that James the stationmaster was in Staines [Middlesex] in 1861 and Colyton [Devon] in 1871.

In addition to this, there is only one James Dermott that I have found on the census of 1851, 1861 and 1871, who is of the right age. Further evidence is provided by the fact that there is only one death of a James Dermott in 1873. We know the stationmaster James died in the JQ 1873 at Axminster age 71.

The pension register which records James Dermott of the 6th Dragoons, shows payment ceased in 1873. There is a note against his name which appears to read Woolwich 1/7. This might suggest that Woolwich was going to be the next place for him to collect his pension. We know Robert and Elizabeth were in Woolwich in 1871, so maybe the intention was to be near his daughter and his grandchildren.

No one could accuse Michael of jumping to conclusions. He always made sure he had all the bases covered. He also had added another generation to the family and that was a real bonus.

Following my theory that James may have been the son of a soldier, he had searched all of the regiments stationed in Guernsey between 1800 and 1802: four infantry regiments, a company of the Royal Artillery and a regiment of Militia. The only Dermott he found was one John Dermott, a Private in the 43rd Regiment of Foot who, along with 13 other men, was discharged on 8 November 1802 and left Guernsey for Weymouth.

Again, you don't have to be on the spot to do military research, although I would never diminish in the slightest the enormous benefit of having someone who was not only on the spot but spot-on as well! Through the mailing list for the genealogical society, I received a couple of links to websites listing children of the military and found a James Dermott and his brother, Thomas (previously unknown), admitted on 4 June 1807 to the Royal Military Asylum (RMA), Chelsea, under the 43rd Regiment of Foot, John's regiment. The children were five and six years old.

The RMA (later called the Duke of York's Military School) was established in 1802 and provided education for both girls and boys of fallen and serving rank-and-file soldiers. It must be remembered that this was during the Napoleonic wars, which lasted from 1793 to 1815, and a million men and boys from the British Isles bore arms during that time. At the Battle of Waterloo there were, according to reports, some 4000 boys aged between 10 and 17 in all the armies that fought and, at the height of the war, the RMA was home to 1500 orphan boys and girls. It was established to replace the dependence of military families on regimental depots and the charity of the officers. Without such provisions, destitute families of soldiers had to rely on the workhouse system, which in those days meant that families had to travel from the regimental depot to the parish in which the father had settlement. Unless the commanding officer of the regiment could provide a signed pass of safe conduct through parishes along the way, the family could have been charged with vagrancy. The asylum (meaning sanctuary) provided the country with the first large-scale system for the education of working-class children. They were taught reading, writing and arithmetic and, well into the

19th century, children leaving the asylum were provided with indentured apprenticeships in all trades and callings. Of course many boys were discharged from the RMA to various regiments, and the Dermott boys were two of those.

From the RMA records we found that James and Thomas were the sons of John and Eleanor Dermott. That was new – a name for their mother. Michael went off to the records office and later sent me photocopies of all the records pertaining to them. They proved fascinating reading.

The earliest mention of John Dermott (sometimes spelled Dearmott, Dearmot, Diarmud, Diarmott and Durmod) was in the Londonderry Regiment of Foot (also called the Londonderry Fencibles) commanded by Lord Viscount Henry Conyngham, who was granted a warrant on 14 January 1795 to *raise as many men in any county or part of our Kingdom of Great Britain* as he could. The regiment was raised in Ireland and almost certainly in Londonderry between January and March 1795.

On the return dated 14 April 1795, a John Durmod is listed on the inspection roll of Lieut Col Napier's Company at Warrington, Lancashire, with the remarks that he was 19 years old, 5ft 7ins tall and came from Ireland. The list began with the names of the sergeants, then corporals, then drummers, before listing the privates in order of height. The tallest of the privates was 5ft 10ins and the shortest 5ft 2ins. The oldest recruit was 50 (a sergeant) and the youngest (a drummer) just 11 years of age and barely 4ft tall. They had obviously been attested previously in Ireland because there were notes against two saying *recruiting in Ireland* and against another saying *sick in London Derry*.

An embarkation return for the regiment shows they arrived at Liverpool on 21 March 1795 and they were in Lancashire from April to June, then in Taunton, Somerset, ending up in Exeter, Devon, in August that year. The August return shows a number of officers on service with the 43rd Regiment. At this time, John Durmod disappeared from the Londonderry Regiment and he reappeared as John Dermott on the draft to 43rd Regiment dated 25 August 1795 at Exeter.

The original musters of the 43rd Regiment for the second half of 1795 show a total of 380 men drafted from the Londonderry Regiment, with a note against a few that said *received from the late Londonderry Regiment,* which meant the regiment had been disbanded. The 43rd were making up its numbers, and by 1797 were up to the full complement of 1000 men. They embarked for the West Indies on 15 March, disembarking at Fort George, Martinique, then moved on to Fort Edward and then St Pierre. On 6 February 1800, less than three years later, they moved back to Fort George, and by that time the regiment numbers had dwindled to below 300, mainly from sickness, and men were allowed to volunteer for other regiments prior to the 43rd being sent home. The remainder of the regiment, including John, embarked from Port Royal, Jamaica, on board HMS *Prince of Wales* on 25 April 1800, landing at Portsmouth on 30 June.

The regiment moved to Gloucestershire in August and was stationed there for the rest of the year. Before returning to the Isle of Wight for embarkation to Guernsey, John married Eleanor Chambers and a few months later their son James was born, and a second son Thomas a year later.

John is shown as discharged on 8 November 1802 on passage to Weymouth in Dorset, however he re-enlisted on 2 March 1803 from the Marlborough district. He moved to Ashford Barracks in Kent in 1804, then to Hythe in Kent in 1805, and in 1807 was at Colchester in Essex with the regiment preparing to embark to Copenhagen, which they did in July 1807. On 4 June, in preparation for their removal overseas, John and Eleanor enrolled their young sons James (born on 12 April 1801) and Thomas (born on 16 April 1802), in the Royal Military Asylum.

James and Eleanor returned from Copenhagen to Colchester in September 1907. They were there until the battalion embarked for Portugal on 1 August 1808 as part of Wellington's Peninsula Army. After their defeat and evacuation at Corunna, John returned to Plymouth on 14 February 1809 and transferred on 26 April to the 2nd Battalion, preparing to embark on the Walcheren Expedition in August 1809. A fleet of 235 ships including 58 warships set sail to capture Antwerp from the French and their 44,000 troops were based on the malaria-infested Walcheren Island (now part of the Netherlands' province of Zeeland). In just eight weeks, the inept British commanders had lost only 218 men in action, but 4000 were dead from illness and another 11,000 were seriously ill. It was an ill-fated and disastrous campaign.

The final quarterly muster for 1809 shows that John Dermott died at Weely, just a few miles from Colchester, on 13 December, most likely one of the seriously ill 11,000. It also confirmed he had enlisted on 13 August 1795, and had one other piece of information – he was born in Ireland in a place called Castletown.

Although his widow Eleanor received John's £4 6s 8d prize money for the two campaigns, she did not take her sons out of the RMA. They stayed there until, at 14 years of age, they too became army men – or should I say army boys. At the RMA they would have been fed, clothed, educated and given the opportunity to go into a trade, or volunteer for the army. It was probably a better life than the one Eleanor could have given them. Not that life in the RMA was all beer and skittles – it actually seemed to be all beer and bread.

The children were given three meals a day. Breakfast was the same every day, being milk pottage 1oz (30g) of oats mixed with 2/3 cup (160ml) milk made to a porridge – plus 1/20 of a quartern loaf (approximately 100g) of wholemeal bread. Dinner was the same amount of bread, plus ½ pint (220ml) beer, 12oz (675g) potatoes and 8oz (450g) of meat, either stewed or roasted. On two days of the week, pea soup or a suet pudding was substituted for the meat. Supper was bread and ½ pint (220ml) of either milk or beer, and four days a week 1½oz (45g) of cheese was added to the diet. There seemed to be absolutely no allowance for fruit or vegetables.

For the sergeants and nurses there was only one meal a day, which consisted of 1lb (500g) each of meat, potatoes and bread, plus a daily allowance of 3 pints (1.3l) of beer. One day a week, pea soup or bacon was substituted for the meat. In addition, the sergeants had 1lb (500g) of cheese and ½lb (250g) of butter weekly, while for the nurses the amounts of butter and cheese were reversed. Why that was so I have absolutely no idea.

James was discharged on 10 August 1815 and Thomas on 26 June 1816, and it is highly unlikely that the brothers had any further contact with each other. Thomas became a trumpeter with 13th Light Dragoons, was sent to India and died there on 11 February 1828 at 25 years of age, the £1 6s 11½d owing to him paid by Will to a William Dixon.

James volunteered for the 6th Dragoons under the Earl of Pembroke as a 14-year-old tailor, 4ft 5¾in (1.36m) tall, with a fair complexion, grey eyes and brown hair. He also became a trumpeter, rising to the rank of Trumpet Major (a sergeant) in 1837 and rising to the height of 5ft 8½in (1.74m) on his discharge on 10 October 1843. He was considered medically unfit for further duties after some 28 years in the army due to *disordered respiration,* which seems to have been a term for asthma, and *general weakness of constitution from years and length of service.*

So now we have army people on both sides of my father's family. On the Dowding side, Frederick James served 12 years, seven of them in India. On the Brown side, Charles' brother Robert James and his father Robert were both military men. Going further, we now knew that Robert's wife Elizabeth Ellen came from an army family, with her father James, her uncle Thomas, and their father John Dermott, all being army men – as was her first husband, Michael Connell. Not that I am dumb, but it took me a while to fall in to the fact that the military connection continues through me. Both the men I married were from army families and both served in the Australian army, one of them in Vietnam.

Methinks far more is carried in the genes than mere physical characteristics.

20. Namesakes

Why, can you imagine what would happen if we named all the twos Henry or George or Robert or John or lots of other things? You'd have to say Robert plus John equals four, and if the four's name was Albert, things would be hopeless.

Norton Juster
'The Phantom Tollbooth', 1961

By this time you probably have become very well aware that names repeat themselves in families. This is partly because of naming patterns but also because, for some reason, people find some names attractive and others not. I would have been astounded if somewhere in the Brown family up popped an Algernon or a Percy, an Adelaide or a Maude.

Of course, the name given is not always the name gone by. An example is Charles' mother Elizabeth Ellen, sometimes listed as Ellen and sometimes as Elizabeth. She was most likely named after her mother Elizabeth, but called by her second name within the family. The same may have been true for Charles' brother Robert James – named for his father Robert, but possibly called James by the family and that may explain why Charles named his father as James on his marriage certificate. If he had known his older brother was named for his father, and if he called his older brother James, it would make sense that he thought his father's name was James too – after all he was only five years old when his father died and he was separated from his mother.

Cousin Liz was named Olive Elizabeth, and while she was known as Olive through her earlier years, later on she started calling herself Liz. Olive is an interesting name in the Brown family. Its first known occurrence is with Olive Ann Dowding born in 1886 – Sarah's sister and witness at her wedding. In the next generation, Sarah named a daughter after her, and her sister Lucy named her youngest daughter Olive Viola. In the following generation, two of Sarah's daughters gave their firstborn the name

Olive, and two generations later, my son named one of his daughters Olivia, not knowing the history of the name within the family.

Another example of the inadvertent re-use of names within the family occurred when my nephew called his daughter Lily. He didn't know it, but his grandfather's older sister was called Lilian. Lilian's second name was May, after her mother's youngest sister, and it wasn't until seven years after Lily was born that we found out she has a middle name – and guess what – it's May. Neither of her parents, who live across the country, knew of the existence of the name Lily in the family and certainly did not know their daughter's great-great aunt was called Lilian May.

Generation 1	Olive Anne DOWDING b 1886	Lilian Martha DOWDING b 1872
Generation 2	Olive Annie DOWDING b 1905 Olive Mae DOWDING b 1910 Olive Viola HOARE b 1913	Lilian May BROWN b 1904
Generation 3	Janet Frances Olive b 19... Olive Elizabeth (Liz) b 19...	
Generation 4		
Generation 5	Olivia Jacqueline b 19...	Lily May b 19...

Of course names get shortened, nicknames are used, and names can be completely changed for one reason or another. Eleanor can be shortened to Ellen, which is also a nickname for Helen. Elizabeth can be Eliza, Bess, Beth, Liza, Lisa, Elise. Ann can be Hannah, Nancy and Nan or even Agnes. Margaret can be Meg, Peggy, Maggie, Rita, Madge, Greta, Marguerite and even Daisy (*marguerite* is the French word for daisy). Mary can be Marie, Maree, Minnie or Polly. As for men's names, John can be Jack, Cornelius can be Neil, Henry can be Harry or Hal, and Francis can be Frank. And that list doesn't even look at European names that have been anglicised.

Sometimes the person who is supplying information, especially about deaths, does not know all there is to know, and sometimes errors of transcription are made. Charles' brother John Nicholson Brown was buried under the name Robert Nicholson Brown – easily explained, as his father's name was Robert and it was probably just a mistake on the part of the chaplain. Other mistakes can be made because of accents or dialects that are written phonetically.

One case that impacted on my research concerned the Tullidge family – but to get to them we need to go back one more generation and look at the family of Elizabeth Ellen's mother, who was born Elizabeth Treves. Treves is an unusual name and I had made a point at an earlier stage in my researches to investigate whether there was any connection between this Elizabeth Treves born in Dorchester, Dorset, and the famous Treves family from the same area.

Sir Frederick Treves, 1st Baronet, surgeon to the King, soldier, author and befriender of Joseph Merrick 'the Elephant Man', was born the son of an upholsterer on 15 February 1853 at 8 Cornhill, Dorchester, in Dorset. He was the 5th child and 3rd son of William Treves and Jane Knight and the grandson of William Treves, cabinet maker, and Elizabeth Greening. William and Elizabeth had six surviving children, two of whom were called (not surprisingly) William and Elizabeth. Son William took over the family business and branched out into upholstering. He became a master cabinet-maker and in 1861 was employing ten men, two women and two boys and was the father of Frederick Treves. Daughter Elizabeth married James Dermott, a Trumpet Major in the 6th Dragoons, and became the mother of Elizabeth Ellen, making Frederick and Elizabeth Ellen first cousins, as they shared the same grandparents.

As we know now, Elizabeth Ellen was widowed twice, was unable to raise her surviving children, spent time in workhouses and lies in an unmarked grave. Her cousin Frederick led a very different life. He and his two brothers William Knight Treves and Edward Treves all became very successful surgeons. How did these three sons of a cabinet-maker and upholsterer move up through the economic and social ranks to the privileged positions they later held? What happened to promote this change in anticipated occupation? Surely one son would have been expected to take on the family business. Well, I think the answer lies in where they were living. On the 1861 census they were still living at 8 Cornhill, Dorchester. Next door, at No. 9, George Curme and his family had moved in. George was, amongst other things, a member of the Royal College of Surgeons. Methinks William saw an opportunity for his sons to better themselves and the boys may have gained a patron of sorts in Dr Curme.

So what happened to the girls of the family? Well, Elizabeth we know married an army man, James Dermott. After he died in 1873, she either did not contact her brother the upholsterer and cabinet maker, or her nephews the surgeons, or she did contact them and they rejected her. We know she was reduced to receiving parish relief because her daughter said so in her settlement statement made in 1880. She, her daughter and four grandsons were all living together in probably very poor conditions at 76 Union Street, Lambeth, in 1881, the year of her death.

Elizabeth had two surviving sisters – Susannah and Frances. Frances Treves never married and became a Deaconess in the church, dying childless in Islington in 1904. Susannah married John Tullidge, farmer, and innkeeper of the Wood and Stone Inn in Dorchester, and she obviously kept in touch with Elizabeth because the 1861 census finds members of the two families living together. James Dermott, then discharged from the army, was a stationmaster living in Ashford, Middlesex, with his wife Elizabeth and their daughter Elizabeth Ellen. With them is Joseph Tullidge, the son of Susannah (Elizabeth's sister), his wife Henrietta and their one-year-old daughter Jane Ellen.

By 1871 James and Elizabeth Dermott had moved with the railways to Colyton, Devon, where James was the stationmaster. John and Susannah Tullidge were still living at the Wood and Stone Inn but their son Joseph and his family had moved to London and were living at 22 Cambridge Terrace, Lambeth.

By 1881 Joseph and Henrietta Tullidge had moved again, this time to 7 Orlando Road, Clapham. I did not know this until I started investigating the Treves family and it was the name Clapham that set off a clanging in my brain. I knew I had come across that suburb before and couldn't remember where. A bit more thought and a bit more rifling through a mountain of handwritten notes and printed emails and I unearthed the reference to Clapham. It was on an email from Judy, setting out the admissions and discharges of Elizabeth Ellen and her boys at the Lambeth workhouse and infirmary. The records showed that Elizabeth Ellen had been discharged to the workhouse from the infirmary after her youngest son Thomas had died in April 1882, and from where, two weeks later on 10 May, she was discharged to *Mrs Dulwich, 7 Holy Andrew Rd, Macauley Rd, Clapham*. I remembered I had tried to find a Mrs Dulwich in Clapham at the time but had absolutely no success, so I had just left it at that. Now the penny dropped.

The significance of the names Dulwich (pronounced *dull-itch*) and Tullidge had not occurred to me when I had seen them written, but when spoken aloud, they sounded so similar that I immediately suspected they were the same family and that this was an error made in the records by the Lambeth workhouse clerk. I looked up both Clapham addresses to see how close they were. The houses in Macauley Road backed on to those in Orlando Road. That was enough for me. Elizabeth Ellen had moved from the workhouse to stay, at least temporarily, with her cousins Joseph and Henrietta Tullidge.

Not unusually, tracing the Tullidge family was not as easy as it sounds – on the 1841 census they were recorded as both Sullidge and Tallidge, and on the 1851 census as Gullidge. When surnames are changed, particularly the first letter or letters, tracing families can be a time-consuming and frustrating business. Because of the way databases work, you normally have to have at least the first three letters right before you start inserting *?* (for a one-letter variation as in *Dow?ing*) or * (as a wildcard to pick up all endings, as in *Isabel** for Isabel, Isabelle, Isabella). With the initial letter, it was just a matter of trying any letter I thought might have been misinterpreted due to the writing style of the enumerator.

With first or given names, the problem mainly lies in either mistranscriptions of middle letters – e.g. confusing *H, W* and *N,* or *I, J, T* and *F*; or the search not picking up short versions of names – e.g. *Thos* for Thomas, *Jas* for James, *Jno* for John, *Wm* for William, *Chas* for Charles. Repetition of names within family groups can be a curse or a blessing, depending on your state of mind. William, son of William, son of William, son of William can be a bit confusing in trying to work out the generations. William, son of George, son of William, son of George can also be confusing if there are other sons in the family called William, making George and William brothers as well as father and son.

To check properly on the extent to which the same names were repeatedly used in my family, I chose the adult descendants of William and Eleanor Nicholson of South Charlton, Robert Brown's great-grandparents. I counted them, their seven children, 14 grandchildren, 16 great-grandchildren and 25 great-great grandchildren. For the 64 people counted, there were only nine different women's names and 12 different men's names – and that included middle names as well as first names.

Five generations of Nicholson names

<u>Women</u>		<u>Men</u>	
Eleanor	Elizabeth	William	Charles (my grandfather)
Mary	Isabella	John	George
Martha	Grace	Robert	Richard
Jane	Hannah	James	Henry
Ann		Michael	Thomas
		Andrew	Alfred

I also looked at the names of the 23 people I had recorded as spouses.

There was a remarkable similarity in their names. There were only five new names overall – Anthony, Phyllis (of which there

were two), Euphemia, Sarah and Charlotte. I didn't count Ellen as
it is a shortened version of Eleanor.

Five generations of Nicholson spouses' names

Husbands	Wives
John	Mary
George	Phyllis
William	Jane
Anthony	Elizabeth
Thomas	Euphemia
	Ellen
	Sarah (my grandmother)
	Charlotte

Although a long way from his family, Robert Brown (Mary
Nicholson's son) had chosen for his children the names Robert,
James, John, Nicholson (his mother's maiden name), Mary,
Charles, George, Alexander, Thomas and Alfred. Only Charles
and Alexander were names not already evident in his family.

Charles, Robert, George, James, John and Alexander were all
names carried in the next generation by Charles' four sons.

21. Lost and Found

Victorian children were very close to death and suffering. In the 1830s almost half the funerals in London were for children under ten years old. Babies were especially likely to become ill, and up to half of all poor children born in London died in their first year.

Peter Bailey, www.ourwardfamily.com

Like millions of other family historians researching families in the UK, I had been anxiously looking forward to the release of the 1911 census. When it became available, I rushed to the website to search the index for Charles and Sarah and my father's siblings. They were living, all seven of them, in the two-roomed Cupar Cottage, at 2 Tovey Place on the corner of Wilkin Street, Kentish Town, very close to the Kentish Town West railway station. They had been married for nine years and had five children, the elder two, Charles and Lilian, were at school.

For Charles' older brother Robert James I could find no definite match, so I sent off another email to Michael to check a few possibilities for me and within a few days got a package of A3-size copies of the actual census pages filled out by the head of the household. My grandmother Sarah had filled out their census paperwork, as Charles would no doubt have been either asleep or at work.

Nestled among the pages, which included census details for various members of my mother's family as well, were three for men called Robert James Brown. They were the only ones who were likely to have been candidates for Charles' brother, being close in age and living in the London area. With the census returns having been filled out and signed by people in their own hand, and as I had army documents that had my Robert James' signature on them, I was able to eliminate two of the three. A close look at the handwriting for the third Robert James Brown, a prison officer born in Maidstone, revealed a certain similarity to our RJB's hand, but it was not a dead ringer, so I looked him up and found his birth in Kent, so he was not ours either.

As none of the Robert James were apparently mine, my next step was to see if I could find a death for a Robert Brown between 1901 – when we know he was living near St John's Wood – and 1911. The only one I saw of the right age who had died in London during those 10 years, died in 1906 in Kensington, which is reasonably close, so I sent off for his death certificate.

Kensington is only 2½ miles (4km) from Kentish Town, where his brother Charles was living in 1911 – although he wouldn't have moved there until after 1906, because his son Robert George was born in Poplar that year. Perhaps Robert James looked Charles up when he got back from India (after all, he would have known no one else). If Robert James died in 1906, maybe the 'long lost brother', who we all assumed was Charles' older brother, was in fact the younger George Alexander (as indicated on my Uncle Jim's hand-drawn family tree).

Anyway – all this speculation might come to nought. I just had to wait until I got the certificate and saw what it had to say. Maybe it would resolve the issue and maybe not – that's the way of family history after all.

Inevitably, the certificate came and, no, he wasn't who I was looking for. This one was simply Robert not Robert James, and he was a metal polisher from Teddington who died of TB. I checked him out and, yes, he had been born in Teddington, so he definitely didn't belong to us.

I was bereft of ideas. If a name is not there, it's just not there, and there's nothing you can do about it. In any case, I was not at all hopeful that he married and had children. A man in his thirties with secondary syphilis would not have been much of a prospect, I fear.

Of George Alexander I had also found not a trace.

I was forced to draw a line under my efforts to find a living Brown relative.

I had, nevertheless, found two living relatives on the Dowding side. That was surely a bonus. In an effort to complete the picture,

I thought I would have a really good go at finding out what happened to the other children of Frederick and Lucy – the ones who didn't survive into adulthood. I made a start by listing all the births of Dowding children between 1871 (when Lucy's first child Esther Jane was born, just weeks after her marriage to Frederick Dowding), and 1889 when I knew she had gone to America. For those 18 years there were only five living children. Her sixth, May, was born in Connecticut in 1891. On May's American birth certificate it stated she was Lucy's 16th child, but 7th living. According to my reckoning, May was her 6th, not 7th, but I thought she might have counted her daughter's child Robert as hers, which would have made up the seven. The family story from both sides of the Atlantic was that she had had 17 children, not 16, so I wondered if there had been another born in America after May.

Genealogical records are progressively being indexed and digitised and the newest release at that time was passenger lists for people entering the UK between 1868 and 1960 from ports outside Europe – fantastic news for me because I should be able to finally find out when the Dowdings returned to England from America. I knew it must have been some time before 1895 because that was when Frederick James had enlisted for the Cheshire regiment. I looked up the records and there they were, on the *Fürst Bismark* having departed on 3 May, 1894 – Frederick, Lucy, Sarah, George, Olive, May, Robert (Lucy's son)… and Ben! That was a surprise. Benjamin had been born before May, and that made seven living children – so she didn't count Robert after all – another confirmation that Robert wasn't her child but her daughter's. As Ben wasn't on the 1901 census, he must have died before then. I found his death, and the certificate revealed that he was only six when he died from *Caries of the Spine. General Tuberculosis*. The TB had got into his bones, poor soul: another victim of crowded and poor living conditions. He died in St Monica's Home Hospital for Sick Children, which was established in 1874 for surgical and medical patients needing a long course of treatment.

At the same time as I ordered Ben's death certificate, I ordered the one for Lucy's first child Esther Jane. She had died from pertussis (whooping cough) at 15 months of age. She had been born in Hertford, where Lucy's parents lived and where Lucy had been staying on the night of the 1871 census. When Esther died, the family was living at 11 Anchor Street in Bermondsey, Surrey. From these certificates and knowing the districts her living children had been born in, I was able to make pretty good guesses from the civil registration indices as to which Dowding children, born within the years I was searching, could have been Lucy's. I then went through and listed the births of Dowding children in those districts between the 1871 and 1881 censuses, and again after the 1881 census until 1889, when Lucy sailed for America. Then I went searching for the deaths of all Dowdings in the same years. For the early ones, no ages at death were given in the records I could search, but for the later years, ages at death were included on the searchable databases.

Having listed them all, I could disregard the names on the list of births that did not appear on the list of deaths. After that, I inserted Lucy's living children in chronological order and marked their names, birth dates and places of registration. I also added to the list the names of three children who died in Watford, where Lucy's family lived, as I thought their deaths might be worth investigating.

I then marked in colour all the months during which Lucy would have been pregnant. In addition to Lucy's six children I knew about who were born in the UK, I had another 11 names from which to choose eight to make the 14 born in England. The 15th and 16th I knew were born in Connecticut. I chose two to start with, based on their names and the length of time between their births, and those born immediately before and after them. I went for Mary Ann born in 1872 who died in 1873 (between Esther Jane and Lucy) and William who was born and died in 1879 (between Sarah and George). Mary was Lucy's mother's name, and William was Frederick's father's name.

158

Births and deaths of Dowding children

Names	Births			Deaths		
	Yr	Qtr	Place	Yr	Qtr	Place
Esther Jane	1871	Q1	St Olave	1872	Q2	St Olave
Mary Ann	1872	Q2	St Olave	1873	Q2	St Olave
Lucy	1873	Q3	St Olave			
Frederick James	1875	Q1	St Olave			
Sarah	1877	Q1	St Olave			
Louisa	1877	Q4	Poplar	1879	Q1	Poplar
William	1879	Q1	Poplar	1879	Q3	Poplar
Minnie	1879	Q4	Poplar	1880	Q4	Poplar
George Reuben	1882	Q3	Poplar			
Hannah	1883	Q3	St Olave	1884	Q1	St Olave
Annie Mildred S	1885	Q3	St Olave			Watford
Charles Harry	1885	Q3	St Olave	1885	Q3	St Olave
Edward James	1886	Q3	St Olave			Watford
Olive Annie	1886	Q3	St Olave			
Charlotte	1888	Q2	St Olave	1888	Q4	St Olave
Alice Hilda	1888	Q2	Watford	1888	Q2	Watford
Stephen	1888	Q2	St Olave	1888	Q3	St Olave
Benjamin	1890	Q2	Ct, USA	1897	Q2	Hendon
May	1891	Q3	Ct. USA			

Yes, I had gambled and won. The family was still living at 11 Anchor St, Bermondsey when Mary Ann died of phthisis (TB again), and William died when they were living in Bromley, where Sarah was born. He died of something Latin. As near as I could make it, and with the help of an online Latin to English translation website, it seemed that he got a bug in his lower intestines that emptied him out, and he probably died of dehydration. He was just 13 months old.

159

Encouraged by my luck and trusting in my logic, I sent for four more death certificates – Charlotte (Lucy's sister's name); Stephen (Frederick had both an older brother and a nephew called Stephen); Charles Harry (Lucy's father was Charles and her brother was Harry); and Hannah. The name Hannah didn't appear anywhere in either Frederick or Lucy's families unless you count Hannah as a form of Ann – and Lucy did have a younger sister Ann.

Charles Harry's was the first certificate to come. Yes, he was one of Frederick and Lucy's and he died aged four months of diarrhoea and *marasmus*, a protein-energy malnutrition. The next three came a few days later, and while they made for sad reading, at least I had the satisfaction of knowing I had guessed right. Hannah died at nine months of tuberculosis. Charlotte died at 11 months of marasmus again, and convulsions she had had for three days. Stephen was born prematurely at seven months and the cause of his death was *inanition* which, according to the dictionary, is *exhaustion, as from lack of nourishment or vitality... the condition or quality of being empty*. With a big sigh, I entered these details on my spreadsheet and looked for the two other children of Frederick and Lucy who would have made May their sixteenth. There were only two possibles: Louisa and Minnie. I ordered their death certificates and sat back to wait. They weren't long in coming, and I had mixed success. Minnie was ours, but Louisa wasn't. Minnie was born in September 1879 and died 11 months later of thrush and diarrhoea.

That made 13 children born in England and the last two in Connecticut. In the Connecticut birth records, Benjamin was listed as Lucy's 15th child and May as her 18th although this was changed to 16th on the birth certificate. Try as I might, I just couldn't find another Dowding child who was born and died in the time frame allowed by the pregnancies and births of all these other children.

It's easier to see the situation when all of the children's births and the months between them are listed.

Frederick and Lucy Dowding's children

Name	Birth	Place	Gap
Esther Jane	Jan 1871	Watford	
Mary Ann	Jul 1872	Bermondsey	18 mths
Lucy	Nov 1873	Bermondsey	16 mths
Frederick James	Feb 1875	Bermondsey	15 mths
Sarah	Jan 1877	Bromley	23 mths
William	Dec 1878	Bromley	23 mths
Minnie	Nov 1879	Bromley	11 mths
		(Still in Bromley on census night 3 April 1881)	
George Reuben	May 1882	Bermondsey	30 mths
Hannah	Jul 1883	Bermondsey	14 mths
Charles Harry	Apr 1885	Bermondsey	21 mths
Olive Annie	Oct 1886	Watford	18 mths
Charlotte	Nov 1887	Bermondsey	11 mths
		(Frederick and Fred to America)	
Stephen	Sep 1888 (2 mths prem)	Bermondsey	10 mths
Benjamin	May 1890	Rockville CT	21 mths
May	Jul 1891	Rockville CT	14 mths

The obvious time to look for another child would be between Minnie and George, i.e. around the first half of 1881, as there is a most unusual 2½ years between their births; but despite numerous attempts, I just couldn't find one.

There weren't any other births registered to a Lucy Dowding in Rockville except for Robert, who was born in Connecticut on 24 May 1890 to Lucy Dowding junior, aged 16, (father un-named) three weeks and two days before his uncle Benjamin was born. The two boys would have grown up together, almost as twins.

Some of the Dowding family in Connecticut, circa 1892
Back: Fred Jr and Sarah
Front: Lucy Jr with Ben on her knee, George, Frederick Sr and Robert

Benjamin died of tuberculosis in England when he was just six years old. Robert was raised by his grandparents until they died and he was incarcerated at the infamous Ladd School in Rhode Island, where he died in 1951, three months before his 61st birthday. His death certificate says he was less than 3ft 11in (under 1.2m) tall. With his height being a result of endocrine glandular disease, it was likely that he was of perfectly normal size until the age of six or seven, when he ceased to grow. Robert's condition certainly didn't shorten his life span. To live there for 35 years, considering the conditions at the school, was quite an achievement. I am hoping that we will be able to gain access to their records in the future. The old mental health department where the records were being archived was moving somewhere else, and until they are settled, we won't have a chance to access them.

So this seemed to be the end of the story, at least for the present. Family stories go on and on – it's just the energy to chase them down rabbit holes that ebbs and flows.

What comes across the years so poignantly is all the lost children. Lucy Dowding lost 11 children, all of them before they were seven. Elizabeth Ellen lost seven of her nine, and those other two, Robert James and my grandfather Charles, were lost to her while they were still children. And this story would have been repeated within family upon family in the 19th century. So sad!

My mother said to me one day, when we were sitting at the table outside having breakfast, that if Elizabeth Ellen, her husband's grandmother, had lived the length of time her own father had lived, she would have been alive to see my brother born. That makes me feel that if I reach out, I can almost touch knowing her.

22. Review

Summer was ending and we were heading into the best time of the year with the mild days, warm breezes and brilliant blue skies of autumn.

I had spent the better part of a day alternatively staring out the window into the garden with its autumn blooms, and reviewing my story after a gap of a couple of months. I got to the part where I was recounting the searches I had made looking for John and Mary Brown in Alnwick in the 1841 census, when I stopped short as I read what I had written about the John Browns in Alnwick who might have been Robert's father. *One was a 14-year-old boy (too young), one a 60-year-old man (too old), and the other a blacksmith, whose age was recorded as 35 (but who could have been any age between 35 and 39 because of the rounding). He had been born in Scotland. I thought he might be a possibility, but he was living in lodgings in Queens Head Yard and there was no sign of a woman with him. I didn't even know if he was single or married. You had to find an individual 10 years later on the 1851 census to get an exact age and their marital status. I tried to locate this John Brown, blacksmith, on the 1851 census but couldn't. He could have died, moved on or gone back to Scotland.*

Well, call me slow if you like, but it was only then that I thought that maybe he was married and maybe his wife was elsewhere at the time of the census. This is what had happened when I failed to find Lucy Dowding senior on the 1901 UK census. I had found her husband Frederick living with their youngest daughter May in Bushey; their other three children, and grandson Robert, as patients; and their mother, eventually, as an 18-year-old monthly nurse born in Walberton, instead of a 48-

year-old monthly nurse born in Watford. Originally, the birthplace was recorded as *Hants, Bournemouth* but that had been crossed out, and *Herts, Watford* written above it. The writing was small but not illegible and carelessness seemed to have been the cause of the mis-transcription. As this was one case where husband and wife were not together on census night, it couldn't possibly be the only one. Maybe John and Mary Brown was another case?

I really needed to check this out, so I interrupted my editing and got straight on to the 1841 census where I found a possible hit – Mary Brown, aged 25. Our Mary had been born in 1812, making her 28 or 29, but the rounding down on the 1841 census would have had her recorded as being 25. She was a servant to William Forster, solicitor, and his wife, and that night she was resident in Fenkle Street, Alnwick (enumeration district No 5), with two other female servants and one male servant.

I then located John Brown, the Scottish blacksmith, resident in a lodging house in Queens Head Yard (enumeration district No 6). He looked to have been aged 36, rounded down by the enumerator to 35, similar to several others on the same page – Mary Fletcher rounded from 57 to 55; Irene Hope from 34 to 30; and Isabella Gibson from 67 to 65. After printing off the description of the enumeration districts and taking a look at them, I went on to Google maps, plugged in Fenkle Street, Alnwick, and asked for directions to Queens Head Yard. It gave me the Queens Head Hotel, 25 Market Street, which was just 200m from Fenkle Street.

The Queens Head, according to its advertising, is the oldest pub in Alnwick.

The Queens Head Hotel is an old established coaching inn, referred to in an indenture of 1777, sharing in the great historical past of the old Northumbrian town of Alnwick with its many traditional trades and crafts, regularly meeting at the old shambles buildings opposite. The Queens Head has always been a regular stopping off point for travelers on the Great North Road...

In the 1840s the yard would have been a part of the establishment and a staging post where, because of the change of horses and repairs needed to coaches, they would have required a blacksmith. I had previously noticed how many smiths lived very near pubs, and the pub next door to the Queens Head, the Crown Inn, also had a blacksmith and his family.

I was sure now I had my John and Mary Brown. Too many coincidences – right names, right ages, right occupation – a smith (don't forget his son was a shoeing smith when he joined the army). Mary was working just around the corner from where John was living. The total number of Mary Browns in Alnwick on the 1841 census was six – one 50-year-old, one 20-year-old, two 15-year-olds, one 12-year-old and this Mary, who was 25 – the only one of suitable age. The reason why Mary was not living with John could be explained by her living-in as a servant maybe one or a few nights a week. Perhaps she was working so they could save to go to Ireland?

I shared this news with cousin Liz, and Michael and Judy in England, and Judy being very cautious suggested that, as I had mentioned to her once, John and Mary might not even have been in Alnwick in 1841, especially as they had left their son Robert with Mary's parents in South Charlton. Although I felt in my bones that I had found them, I really needed to be able to persuade her by research and logic before I could claim them as my own. I revisited old files and did some more searching, then sent her my argument.

I had previously looked for John and Mary in the 1841 census all over Northumberland. Sixty-eight John Browns born between 1800 and 1810 were living in that county, but only five were with a Mary who could have been a wife, and none of these Marys was the right age – because we know ours was born in 1812. Two were in the Newcastle-upon-Tyne area and three were in Tynemouth. There was also a John and Maria in Tynemouth but also the wrong age. I originally thought that John might have been a widower as there was a John Brown with children Eleanor, George and Robert (aged four) living in Byker, Newcastle, but once I found our Robert listed as a Nicholson, I dismissed them.

I hadn't gone any further afield. Rightly or wrongly I felt that if John and Mary were in another county they would have taken Robert with them. I had hoped I might find the couple off somewhere, with a relative perhaps, with Mary having another baby, but never had I considered them being apart on census night although there was no reason why they shouldn't have been.

I also had another look at John and Mary's marriage certificate, and the witnesses were Ann (her sister) and John (her father) plus a Joseph Robertson. I had looked him up before to see if John and/or Mary were perhaps living with him, but in the light of this new discovery, I thought I would check him out again. There was only one Joseph Robertson in Alnwick on the 1841 census. He was a 25-year-old journeyman joiner, living at Bondgate-Within-Yard 49. The next place on the census was the White Swan Inn, so I looked that up and checked out how far away that was from the Queens Head... 200 m! That was the candle on the cake as far as I was concerned... just too many coincidences.

Out of curiosity I traced Joseph Robertson, and in 1851 found him employed as an assistant joiner by Isabella Reid, a widow, a joiner, and a farmer of 50 acres employing three men. Her unmarried daughter Isabella, and 13-year-old granddaughter Eleanor, were living with her. The next census showed Joseph and Isabella Robertson (the widow Reid's daughter, now married to Joseph) living in Alnwick. Joseph was recorded as being born in *Alnwick (White House)*. Now that certainly rang a bell with me! Having researched all the Browns and Nicholsons in the Alnwick area, I had found a family which came from a place called White House Folly. White House is in the Abbey Lands township in the parish of Alnwick and less than 2kms from South Charlton. So that was the clincher. Joseph Robertson, witness at the marriage, was born just 2kms from South Charlton, where Mary was born and raised. Maybe John Brown even met Mary through his mate Joseph, who was working at the inn around the corner.

I emailed Judy:

"Good enough for me...good enough for you?"

She sent back:
"Yes, definitely good enough for me."

As I had found neither John nor Mary (nor Robert) on the 1851 or any subsequent census returns, I believe they went to Ireland some time between 1841 and 1851. John, being from Scotland, may have had family or other connections there. The Celts of Scotland and Ireland historically travelled pretty freely between the two countries (only 25kms apart at their least distance), as witnessed by the similarity of family names in the two countries.

As for John Brown's occupation, claimed as publican by his son Robert on his marriage certificate in 1866, if the John Brown in Newcastle whom I originally thought was ours was a smith-turned-publican, why could not this John Brown have followed the same path? Being a blacksmith and working for a coach and public house he certainly would have known all about the work.

I don't think I will ever be able to trace John Brown the Scottish blacksmith. I have no idea whereabouts in Scotland he came from because the 1841 census did not give that data, although it was probably from the border. Nevertheless, I felt very settled to know that the Browns did actually hail from Scotland. My father and one son have both visited Scotland and felt very connected to the place. I don't know if I would, but maybe on my next and possibly final trip to the UK I might find out.

I was pleased to know that John was still alive when his son married in 1866, which would have made him around 61 years of age – a good age for his times. His grandson Charles lived to be almost 94 – a very good age for his times. His great-grandson Alexander is still going strong at 90. It looks good for me.

While I was in the revision mood and having tinkered around in the Brown family history again, I thought I would try one last time for Robert James. I opened up the *freebmd.org.uk* website and started a query for the death of a Robert James Brown anywhere in England for the period 1901-1911. They now have an almost complete transcription of the available records for that period – a few are missing from 1904 and 1910 but for all other years, 100% of records have been transcribed. There were only five Robert James Brown deaths that came up in the search, and their ages ranged from 0 to 34. The oldest was a man whose death was registered in 1909 in the Kensington district. St Ann's Terrace, St John's Wood, was where Robert was living in 1901. I remembered that Robert James had shed a couple of years when he joined up, no doubt adopting the workhouse records of his birth year as being 1871 instead of 1869, so, despite the disparity in age, this was a certificate definitely worth sending for. As previously explained, I had learned not to be too pedantic about ages.

The certificate would come in due course. In the meantime, I had a look at whether there was still a hospital in Kensington. I found the present St. Charles Hospital in Exmoor Street was originally built in 1878–81 by the Guardians of the Poor Law Union of St Marylebone as an infirmary for their sick and poor, and in 1909 was called the St Marylebone Infirmary. St Ann's Terrace was also only two miles from Exmoor Street. Hmmmm! Sounded a promising place for a poor and infirm veteran with malaria and syphilis to end his days, but I would just have to wait to see what the certificate said. If this was Robert James, and if he had lived there until 1909, he would only have been two miles away from where Charles and his family moved to some time between September 1906 and July 1909, when their youngest daughter was born.

The certificate arrived and with it came disappointment. I sent this message to England:

Well, I received the death certificate of Robert James Brown who died in Kensington in 1909 and unfortunately he is not ours. This one was born in the Marylebone workhouse and died a 'general porter' at the Marylebone infirmary of pneumonia & pleurisy and something else I can't decipher but it certainly isn't either malaria or syphilis, which I suspect would have been mentioned in the case of our RJB.

169

After an enquiry from Judy, who asked how I knew he was born in the Marylebone workhouse, I emailed her the scanned certificate and she had a look at it with different eyes. She thought the certificate said *General Porter **from** Marylebone workhouse* not *General Porter **born** Marylebone workhouse*. I looked again and agreed with her. She undertook to check the records of the workhouse and see if she could get some more details on this Robert James Brown. A couple of months passed and I hadn't heard back, so I emailed again with an enquiry as to how she had got on with the records. It so happened she had forgotten to check them out, but did so immediately and sent this information back.

> *I have found the death of Robert James BROWN in the Marylebone Infirmary. The entry in the death register adds nothing to what you already know.*
> *The Infirmary's Admission/Discharge register adds more detail.*

St Marylebone Board of Guardians –
Infirmary Admission and Discharge Register,
1909 Sep-1910 Sep

Date of admission:	*3 Dec 1909*
No. of admission:	*4864*
Name:	*Robert J Brown*
Sex:	*M*
Age:	*34*
Calling:	*Porter, ex-soldier*
Religious Creed:	*C.E.*
Name & address of nearest relation:	*No Friends*
Observations, general remarks:	*Single, nil*

> *I thought you would like **ex-soldier**. But I am concerned at the lack of any named relations. If this is our man, why did he not name his brother Charles?*
> *The death certificate says (in the Occupation column) General Porter from Marylebone Workhouse. I had thought this implied that this RJB was on the workhouse staff. So I*

checked all the staff records that I could find for the Board of Guardians at this period, but I did not find him listed anywhere. This is strange because these registers look very comprehensive. They were compiled annually, and they list the names of workhouse staff, starting at the top with the Guardians themselves, right down to the 3rd Boiler Stoker (temporary). They do include several porters.

I now wonder if perhaps this RJB wasn't actually employed by the workhouse, but was employed as a general porter elsewhere and was in the workhouse, albeit temporarily, when he was taken ill and transferred to the infirmary? I must say that is not how I read the death certificate at first, and it would not be usual to find this in the occupation column. But it is strange not to find him in these apparently comprehensive staff lists.

I could check the main Marylebone workhouse admission/discharge registers, in case he was admitted as an inmate, but unfortunately I ran out of time today -- as ever. But I will have another go at this, because it would be good if we could find something more to help us identify this man. It seems to be close, but perhaps not quite close enough? I'll be interested to hear your views.

I dashed off a reply.

What news! I am excited indeed by the words "ex-soldier". What we have is a single ex-soldier working as a porter who was admitted to the Marylebone infirmary 10 days before his death from pneumonia.

To explain the non mention of any family, RJ was originally discharged from Anerley House on 3 Jan 1887 to Mr Beal, baker, of West Wickham, Kent and his brother Charles on 1 Oct 1889 to Mr Thomas, baker, of Penge. Family lore has it that the brothers met only once after RJ had joined the army, which he did on 30 July 1890.

171

At the 1891 census, Charles was living at 332 York Rd, Wandsworth as assistant baker to Mr Provins and according to his army medical record, RJ was at Aldershot that night.

RJ left for India on 4 Nov 1897. I don't know where Charles was living at that time but by 1901 he was boarding at 39 West Ferry Rd, Milwall prior to his marriage later that year. He was working for J Lyons & Co at Cadby Hall in Hammersmith and RJ may have had no clue as to where he was. RJ might have tried to get in touch with Charles on his return from India, as he was so ill, but if he hadn't kept in contact by letter (unlikely because my grandfather certainly was no letter writer) he may have had no way of tracking him down.

Perhaps the records of the Marylebone workhouse will provide the information we need to nail RJ. I certainly hope so because I think this could well be him.

Fingers crossed!

Well, the records of the Marylebone workhouse did nail him. Judy turned up his settlement certificate which proved it.

St Marylebone Board of Guardians
STMBG 165/25
Examinations as to Settlement (9 Feb 1904 - 31 Dec 1905), p 231
[undated]
Robert James Brown, 30
S. A. [= Salvation Army]
Molyneux Street, 3 wks
Was sent by Wandsworth to N. Surrey Dist School Anerley, W. Penge
Left there when 15 or 16
Apprenticed (Baker) to Mr Bell, West Wickham for 18 months

No settled address since.

[marginal note]: *West Wickham? Mr Bell not at West Wickham as Baker at present time!*

There it was – absolutely irrefutable proof. Anerley... apprentice baker... Mr Bell (for Bell read Beal)... West Wickham. No mention of the army, but that didn't matter because Judy had gone further and delved into the admission and creed registers.

Only one workhouse admission/discharge register survives for the relevant period. The details below are taken mainly from the Creed Registers covering May 1904 - Sep 1910.

Robert James Brown was first admitted to the St Marylebone workhouse (Northumberland Road) on 21 May 1904, from the Salvation Army Shelter, and was described as single, and destitute. That is probably when the above examination notes were taken, though they are not dated. He was a regular "in-and-outer" at the workhouse for the next year or so, discharged and readmitted the same day on a more-or-less weekly basis until April 1905.

Then followed a gap of about two years, and he was readmitted on 21 May 1907. He was again discharged and readmitted weekly until 5 Dec 1907. He returned for a few days in Feb 1908, and was then in the house more-or-less continuously from 17 Sep 1908 until 3 June 1909, when he was admitted to the Infirmary. From 28 Aug 1909 he was back in the workhouse until 3 Dec 1909, when he went back to the Infirmary. As we know, he died there 10 days later, on 13 Dec 1909.

The registers are inconsistent as to his name (Robert, and Robert James), his age (ranging from 23 to 45 over a five-year period), and his occupation (baker, painter, porter). But I am convinced by the way the admissions/ discharges are arranged that this is all the same man -- each

173

time readmitted from the Salvation Army shelter by the same Relieving Officer (Mr Twyer).

The only other Robert Brown recorded in the workhouse during these years is Roman Catholic, married, and has an age range of 68 to 90 over the same five-year period. Again he is clearly the same man each time, as he is accompanied on several occasions by his wife Julia of similar age.

So there we have it. This looks like definitive closure for RJB.

Once again your persistence has paid off, but once again it is a very sad outcome.

I read and re-read the news from Judy. I felt good about having tied up Robert James's life but very sad too, for this solitary man, diseased and battling.

Sometime between September 1906 and when Robert James died, Charles and the family had moved from Poplar (now Tower Hamlets) to Holmes Road in Kentish Town, and within five kilometres (three miles) of the Salvation Army hostel where his brother was living. What a shame they had lost contact. Robert James had no one to call on in his many hours of need. How sad, too, that he died alone with no named friends, and not knowing his family. He was always remembered by the family and it was he, of course, who started Liz and me looking for lost but living relatives.

It seemed now that I had exhausted all possible avenues in the search for the Brown family. There was only George Alexander unaccounted for, and to find him... well, that was about as likely as winning Lotto.

Part of trying to tie up loose ends in this eight-year journey to find my grandfather's family was in revisiting lots and lots of email correspondence, and trying to put it in files relating to its main topic. I'm not a very dedicated filer and often leave these things to do in the hot holiday weather of January. It was thus in doing this chore, which I had left for two years instead of just one, I discovered an email from cousin Liz about George Alexander that she had sent me back in 2007. She had been looking for him, once again, in the 1891 census, which lists over 400 George Browns of the right age, but in the database she had searched, it very helpfully listed 'household, institution or vessel' in the first column. She told me:

I went down the lot and looked at all the Institution ones and, surprisingly, there weren't all that many. I just looked at London ones, and besides the Sutton-at-Hone lad (which we have established is definitely not one of ours), there was a George Brown listed as a patient in St Thomas' Hospital in Lambeth. His age is given as 15 and occupation as labourer. I checked the deaths for George Browns of the right age in that area for 1891 and there isn't one, so presumably whatever he was suffering from, he recovered.

Well, I thought I should follow it up because, although Liz had said she would do it when she wasn't so busy, I hadn't heard any more and it probably had slipped down the priority list. I emailed Judy to see what she had to say, and she was quite interested because the boy's birthplace was listed as Battersea. There are some resources for St Thomas' Hospital, and, although the admission registers were destroyed by bombing in 1940, there is a register of in-patients which covers the period between January 1890 and December 1891 when young George was there. A quick check of the 1881 census showed half a dozen George Browns born between 1874 and 1878 in Battersea, which was part of the Wandsworth & Clapham Union. Our George Brown was born in the West Indies in 1878 and disappeared after being discharged from Norwood Schools on 21 July 1882, aged four. The Norwood Schools were run by the Lambeth Union, and Lambeth was where George's mother and brothers initially entered the workhouse system. They were charged back to the Wandsworth & Clapham Union because their mother was born in Wandsworth and that was her place of settlement.

This George was definitely worth looking at, if only for elimination purposes. I spent a few hours on *ancestry.com* and thought I had found the identity of George Brown of Battersea, patient at St Thomas' Hospital. He was probably the son of John and Catherine Brown. John was a lawyer in 1881 and they had two children by then: George and younger brother, John (aged 2). John was with them in 1891 (aged 10) but there was no sign of George. I sent this information to Judy in England and she traipsed along to the records office and came back with:

Not good news, I'm afraid. The Register of Patients for St Thomas' Hospital for 1890-1891 is classified as Unfit, which means that I couldn't look at it. Quite a few registers at that period are in poor condition, and many don't survive at all. I had been hopeful for this one, but all in vain.

I had a good look through the catalogue for St Thomas', but found nothing else that I thought would give any patient details of the sort we need.

Sorry, back to the drawing board.

Well, that was it, I decided. I had to draw a line under this family at some time and I seemed to have reached that point. Perhaps, one day, something might turn up in relation to George Alexander. He is our last hope to find some living relatives on the Brown side. As it stands, only two of Elizabeth Ellen's nine children made it to adulthood and only one of those, my grandfather, married and had a family of his own.

So, despite having found no long-lost Brown relatives, we now know a lot more about where we come from and how fortunate we are to be here. My grandfather lost his whole family when he was still a child, and his own family was of paramount importance to him. He never forgot us, out here in Australia, and kept his promise that his youngest son would share in his estate. When he died and his house was sold, Dad was sent his share.

23. Speaker for the Dead

To understand who a person really was, what his or her life really meant, the speaker for the dead would have to explain their self-story – what they meant to do, what they actually did, what they regretted, what they rejoiced in. That's the story that we never know, the story that we never can know –

Orson Scott Card, 'Speaker for the Dead',1991, p. x

Dear Grandad

I want to tell you about your family – and you can blame Jim for starting what I am about to say.

Around 1984, Jim started a search for information about your father. The only things he had to go on were that your father was called James Brown (from your marriage certificate), and that he was a soldier who had died in India when you were very young. The only record he found that fitted the bill was for a James Brown of the 1st West India Regiment who had died in December 1882 in Sierra Leone from phthisis (which none of us had ever heard of but which we discovered is tuberculosis). The army records didn't show this James Brown as being married however, and Jim wasn't able to get any further. He sent Dad a copy of the death certificate for this man and all of us accepted that this was your father. We were wrong, but it took a long time to find that out.

While he was foraging around in the records, Jim also turned up some certificates relating to your in-laws, the Dowdings. He found Grandma's birth certificate and her parents' marriage certificate. He also tracked down some other Dowdings – some of whom were our family and some of whom, as it turned out, were not.

Jim sent copies of these birth and marriage certificates to Dad, along with some explanatory notes about his researches, and Dad showed them to me. Being of a rather inquisitive nature and one who doesn't like any loose ends, I tried to fit a few pieces together that Jim had found puzzling but, not being able to just pop into the

English archives from Western Australia, and having other priorities at the time, I put it all aside.

I can't remember what really started me researching your family in earnest, but suffice it to say that it was nearly 20 years later when I engaged Jim's daughter Judy, and Lil's daughter Liz (Olive), in the quest. I had become aware that family was very important to me and I wanted to find out if we had any living but 'long lost' Brown relatives. I knew about the story of you and your older brother being orphaned and you losing touch with him after he left the workhouse, and it seemed to me that someone should try to find out what happened to him. These days there is a huge interest in family history. I don't exactly know why, but perhaps as we have become much more affluent, and as we now rely so much on technology to replace human-to-human communication, we have become increasingly isolated from each other. Our children live their own lives very early now, and parents and children, even in the same house, are often very cut off from each other. I think the isolating impact of technology has spawned a desire to be connected to others, and the others who we are most connected to are our families.

These days we have a lot of technology that is able to do amazing things – things that astound me, and that you would find difficult to comprehend, I am sure. Like most things, this technology is a double-edged sword. It has benefits and drawbacks. On the one hand it tends to isolate people from each other but on the other hand it has given people the ability to access almost anyone and anything worldwide instantly. It is this technology and the generous assistance of others that has allowed me to reach back into the last 200 years and find your family.

Despite a bit of a head start Jim had given me on the Dowding side of the family, I was really most interested in finding out what happened to your brother and whether he survived, married and had children. Dad is the last of his generation still with us and I asked him and all your grandchildren I had contact with if they knew anything more than I did about your early life, but no one seemed to know much about you at all. Even Dad couldn't tell me much. Judy had some handwritten notes Jim had made for her, and from them I learned that you, with your older brother, had grown up in a place called Anerley House. Dad told me it was in Penge, in Surrey. Apart from that, there was nothing I was told that I didn't already know from family stories.

Like Jim, I started my search in India, looking for some record of your birth, and like Jim, had absolutely no success. Then I tried finding your mother in the records of deaths at sea but, again, had no success. Trying to identify a Mrs Brown (first name unknown), who died on board an un-named ship on an unknown date and was presumably buried at sea, then positively linking her to you, was just not possible. I didn't know your father's regiment, and trying to find him without it was out of the question. The only other thing I could do was to try to track down some records of Anerley House where you and your brother (name also unknown) were sent. It was there that I eventually had some success.

By that time, Liz and I had been working on your family for a couple of years, chasing down a lot of dead ends. With 'Anerley House' we were on a winner, although we didn't know it at first. I'm sure this will come as a surprise to you that both your father and your mother died in England – and while we're talking about surprises, you were the third of their six children. Now I don't know if you had any memory of your siblings other than your older brother because you were only six or seven when you last saw them, but not a whisper about any other children came down to any of the grandkids. Judy did come across a hand-drawn family chart Jim had done and it showed not an older brother, but a younger brother, named George. None of us know how or why Jim had put a name to this brother of yours but it turned out he was quite correct.

So, let me take a deep breath and start from the beginning.

Grandad, your father was a soldier, as you knew, but he was with the British, not Indian Army, and served in the West Indies, not India. He was a sergeant in the Royal Artillery and his name was Robert Brown, not James Brown. He was a 'Geordie', having been born in a little village called South Charlton near Alnwick up

179

in Northumberland. His mother was a local girl called Mary Nicholson, the daughter of a joiner, and his father (your grandfather) was a Scottish blacksmith called John Brown. While your father was still quite a young child I think, the family moved to Ireland. Why this was so, when at this time (the 1840s) everyone was getting out of Ireland, I just don't know. Your grandfather John Brown was a smith employed at the Queens Head at Alnwick on the Great North Road. I would have thought there would have been plenty of work for him there, as it is still running as a 'coach and public house' to this day. Maybe he had family in Ireland, as many in Scotland did, and that is why they went. Anyway, so many Irish records were destroyed in 1922 during the Civil War that I may never find out what happened to the family, or whether your father had any younger brothers and sisters born over there. There certainly were no others born in England.

The reason that I know your grandparents John and Mary Brown went to Ireland is because your father enlisted in the army from Dublin when he was 22. He had followed the trade of his father and was a shoeing smith. From Dublin he was shipped to England, and in England he met and married your mother Elizabeth Ellen Dermott. She was the daughter of James Dermott, also a soldier, from Irish stock, and Elizabeth Treves from Dorset. Elizabeth was aunt to the surgeon Frederick Treves, who performed the emergency appendix operation on Edward VII just two days before his scheduled coronation. No doubt you remember that. I bet at the time you would never have had any idea that the man who saved the King's life was your mother's cousin.

When they married in 1866, your father was a corporal in the Royal Artillery and your mother was a young widow whose two children by her first marriage had died in infancy. Robert and Ellen (as she was called) had six children altogether. I wonder if you remembered her name. I think you probably did because all three of your daughters were named for someone in the family, and Lucy's second name was Ellen.

Your brother Robert James was the oldest – and the only one apart from you who we know survived his childhood. He was named for his father (Robert) and his mother's father (James). Perhaps you confused which of his names was your father's? It would be easy to get that wrong, seeing as you were only five years old when your father died, and just six when you were separated from your mother – but I'm getting a bit ahead of myself here.

The next child born they named John Nicholson. His two names came from his grandfather (John) and from his mother's family name (Nicholson). The Nicholson family hailed from the little village of South Charlton in Northumberland, where your father was born. It was quite a large family, as was usual for those times, and many of the men were joiners and carpenters. That, too, might have come down in the family, as Dad became a carpenter/joiner. Both Robert James and John Nicholson were born while the family was still in England.

Robert and Ellen's only daughter, your sister Mary, was born in Halifax, Canada, after they had been posted there early in 1873. She was named for John's mother and only lived 13 days, poor little pet. She was born on 25 September 1874 – exactly a year before you. Your birth date was not 1 August as you thought, but 25 September 1875 and you, too, were born in Halifax.

When you were only seven months old, the family departed for St Georges in Bermuda, part of the 'West India' group of islands. What we now call the West Indies, your mother called West India, and that is probably where you got the notion you were born in India, then referred to as East India or the East Indies. You were in Bermuda for five years until your father, who had tuberculosis, was repatriated home in November 1880. He must have been very sick on board ship because he died on 15 December, just two days after reaching the garrison station hospital at Portsea Island. Perhaps this was the experience you remembered of someone dying on board ship. That must have been the last time you saw your father.

While you were in Bermuda, two other children were born – your younger brothers George Alexander and Thomas Alfred. When I found out George's second name and remembering Jim's rough family tree with a younger brother George on it, I wondered if you had ever mentioned anything in passing about young George. I like to think that somewhere in the deep dark recesses of your memory, something rang a bell and Alexander seemed a good name for your youngest child.

When your father died, your mother and her four boys were stranded in England in mid-December after five years in the tropical West Indies. How foreign must that have felt for you all – especially you children who had never known anything of England, its climate or social structure. You had no father, no home and no friends. You no longer belonged in the British Army, and the only support your mother got was a warrant to travel to London, where her mother, now a widow, was eking out an existence as a seamstress in Lambeth, receiving assistance from the parish. With nowhere else to go, your mother and her four young boys moved in with her.

When your grandmother Elizabeth Dermott died less than a year later, and with two of her boys sick, your mother took you all to the Lambeth workhouse where she and the two young ones were admitted to the infirmary. You and Robert were sent off to Norwood Schools, and when George got better he joined you there. Little Thomas didn't recover though, and he died in the infirmary. Your mother discharged herself from the workhouse after Thomas died and went to find work. She obviously couldn't support you all, and after nearly a year at Norwood, the three of you were discharged. Robert was sent to Anerley House, while you were sent to St James School in Tooting for a year. After that, you were sent to Anerley House too. You were nearly eight by then.

I'm really sorry that I haven't been able to find out what happened to your brother George. He wasn't sent to Anerley House, and I've looked and looked for him with no success. Maybe someday someone might turn up some information about what happened to him but in the meantime I like to think someone took a shine to him and he was adopted by them and grew up to have a long and happy life.

It was during your time at Anerley that your mother died. She had gone back to the Royal Artillery's headquarters and was living and working in Woolwich. She did not remarry but gave birth to another son William Thomas, on 4 September, 1883. I think she must have been very lonely without her boys and wanted very much to have another child. William Thomas was only two and a half when your mum died and he was bundled off to the Plumstead workhouse. He got sick and was transferred to the infirmary six months later and was there until he died, aged four.

Your mum died of a ruptured aneurism of the aorta on 2 May 1886. She must have told her landlady about you and Robert because the Coroner sent for you both to identify her body and to attend her funeral. There are records that show you were both taken from Anerley to Woolwich to do that. I think that must be where you saw your mother laid out with her black hair all around her. You were 10 years old and the same age as Dad was when Olive died. Perhaps that was why you didn't let Dad go to her funeral – you always said funerals weren't for children. I want to tell you that Liz and I paid a visit to your mother's grave in 2007 and laid flowers on it. We left a little note there in remembrance of her.

When your brother Robert was discharged from Anerley House to be apprenticed to a baker at the beginning of 1887, you were 12 and he was 18. Somewhere in the workhouse system he lost a couple of years in age and was recorded as being only 16. His time as a baker didn't last long and it was probably inevitable that he left to join the army. It was the only life he had known until he was 11, and life in England couldn't have been the best for him. He tried for the Royal West Kents first but was rejected because of his poor eyesight. He tried again with the Royal Artillery three weeks later and this time was successful. He became a driver with the Royal Horse Artillery and at the end of 1897 was posted to India. He was not a big chap, nor a very healthy one, and had numerous

183

bouts of various illnesses for which he was hospitalised, both in England and in India. Finally his health was such that he was sent home in January 1900 and discharged unfit for further service. He was given a small pension for the next 27 months and went to live in St John's Wood.

Robert James died of pleurisy and pneumonia on 13 December 1909 at the St Marylebone Hospital in Kensington, just two miles away from St John's Wood. He was only 40. He had been shuttling back and forth between St Marylebone workhouse and the nearby Salvation Army shelter for the previous five years, the records describing him as *single and destitute*, so we know for certain he had never married and never had any children. I find it so sad that he died not knowing that his family had never forgotten him and that you were living only a few miles away, in Kentish Town.

I wish I had better news for you about your brothers. One of the things that kept me searching for your family was the thought that perhaps I would uncover a living relative, perhaps a grandchild of this long-lost brother of yours I had always known about. It was not to be however. Despite such sadness in your family, it is wonderful to know where the Browns came from, how adventurous they were and how amazing it was that you survived all that you did.

As I write this letter, your youngest son, my own father, is in his 91st year and his target is to live longer than you did. He says you hoped he would live to be 100 and you would come to his funeral. Well, Grandad, I think he will – and yes, you will be there with us too.

With love, respect and admiration,

Gus' girl.

Charles Brown – the last photo

The Old Man Himself

Selected References

Books, periodicals, articles, directories and newspapers
A History of the Parish of St James, South Charlton
Booth's Poverty Map of London, 1898-99
Holmes, Richard. Redcoat. The British soldier in the age of horse and musket. Harper Collins, 2001.
Kentish Independent Newspaper, May 1886
Kentish Mercury Newspaper, May 1886
Kitzmiller, John. In Search of the Forlorn Hope: A Comprehensive Guide to Locating British Regiments and Their Records (1640 to WWI). Vols I & II. Manuscript Pub Foundation, 1988
Lomas, Janis. 'Delicate duties': issues of class and respectability in government policy towards the wives and widows of British soldiers in the era of the Great War. Women's History Review, Volume 9, Issue 1, 2000 pp123-147
London A-Z Directory
PRO Information Sheet. Army Other Ranks: Finding the Regiment.
Rockville Connecticut USA Directories, 1890-1894
Woolwich Gazette, May 1886

Family history centres, libraries and collections
Centre for Kentish Studies, Kent, UK
Greenwich Heritage Centre, Kent, UK
Latter Day Saints Family History Centre, Dianella, Western Australia
National Archives, London, UK
National Children's Home, London, UK
North West Kent Family History Society, Kent, UK
Northumberland Collections Service, Woodhorn, Northumberland
Oriental and India Office Collection, British Library, London
Public Records Office, Kew, Surrey, UK
Western Australian Genealogical Society Inc, Bayswater, Western Australia

Major websites
1901censusonline.com
1911census.co.uk
achart.ca
ancestry.com
booth.lse.ac.uk
british-history.ac.uk
ellisisland.com
wikipedia.org
familysearch.org
freebmd.org.uk
freepages.genealogy.rootsweb.ancestry.com/~hughwallis/
genesreunited.co.uk
genuki.org.uk
gro.gov.uk
google.com
googlemaps.com
kzwp.com/lyons
nationalarchives.gov.uk
nationaltrustnames.org.uk
regiments.org
rootsweb.ancestry.com
workhouses.org.uk

Records, documents and transcriptions, microfiche
Army
British Army location records
British Army register books of births, baptisms, deaths and marriages
Chelsea Pensioner registers
Depot Description books
Overseas returns – Army Chaplains' returns
Regimental Births for India – Madras, Bengal, Bombay
Royal Artillery muster rolls
Royal Military Asylum records 1805-1816
War Office records

WWI US draft records

Births, Marriages, Deaths
General Register Office records of births, marriages and deaths from 1837
Marriages in Northumberland 1813-1837
Overseas returns – Consular, Ecclesiastical, Miscellaneous Foreign Returns, Miscellaneous Foreign Deaths
Registrar General of Shipping and Seamen

Census
UK Census 1841, 1851, 1861, 1871, 1881, 1891, 1901, 1911
US Census 1880, 1900, 1910, 1920, 1930

Parish
Alnwick parish records of baptisms 1700-1849, marriages 1647-1869 and burials 1728-1822
Ellingham parish records 1695-1942.
International Genealogical Index

Workhouse
Apprentice Indentures Woolwich 1884-1927 and Apprentice and Servants Registers for Wandsworth & Clapham Union 1881-1899
Board of Guardians records for Wandsworth & Clapham 1881-1885, Woolwich 1883-1888 and Lambeth 1880-1887
Creed Registers for Westminster, Lambeth 1873-1886 and Wandsworth & Clapham Unions 1880-1895
North Surrey School District admission and discharge records 1883-1889
South Metropolitan School District records: Sutton 1872-1897, Herne Bay 1881-1897, Witham Essex 1882-1896
School Records for Westminster 1867-1912, Lambeth 1850-1893 and Wandsworth & Clapham Unions 1878-1882
Workhouses and Infirmary records for Lambeth 1878-1888 and Woolwich Unions 1880-1895

Printed in Australia
AUOC011329091111
250794AU00002B/1/P